#25-04 BK BUd A

ANIMAL EXPERIMENTATION

Other Books in the At Issue Series:

ANIMAL EXPERIMENTATION

David M. Haugen, *Book Editor*

David L. Bender, *Publisher*

Bruno Leone, *Executive Editor*

Bonnie Szumski, *Editorial Director*

David M. Haugen, *Managing Editor*

An Opposing Viewpoints® Series

Greenhaven Press, Inc.
San Diego, California

Library of Congress Cataloging-in-Publication Data

Animal experimentation / David M. Haugen, book editor.
        p.   cm. — (At issue)
    Includes bibliographical references and index.
    ISBN 0-7377-0149-8 (lib. bdg.). —ISBN 0-7377-0148-X (pbk.)
    1. Animal experimentation—Moral and ethical aspects.
2. Animal experimentation—United States. I. Haugen, David,
1969– . II. Series: At issue (San Diego, Calif.)
HV4915.A635   2000
179′.4—dc21   99-27264
                                                                   CIP

©2000 by Greenhaven Press, Inc., PO Box 289009,
San Diego, CA 92198-9009

Printed in the U.S.A.

Table of Contents

Introduction

For the past three decades, there has been widespread debate over the use of animals in medical science and product testing. Heartrending images of caged monkeys awaiting vivisection in government laboratories and rabbits with skin lesions where cosmetics have been tested convince many that animal research is cruel and often unwarranted. Yet a belief in using every method available to ensure product safety and improve human health keeps a majority of people (53 percent in 1995) in support of animal experimentation. The controversy has succeeded in forcing animal researchers, animal rights activists, and the general public to consider the ethical as well as the practical concerns of experimenting on animals to benefit humans.

Triggering the debate

One of the first events that prompted debate concerning animal experimentation was the 1975 publication of Peter Singer's book, *Animal Liberation: A New Ethics for Our Treatment of Animals*. Singer, an Australian philosopher, questioned whether the information gathered from animal experimentation justified the amount of suffering imposed on research animals. In his view, scientists rarely ever considered achieving such a moral balance. Scientists who failed to address this concern, in Singer's opinion, were perpetrating "speciesism"—a form of racism in which humans ignore the interests and sufferings of animals simply because they are not humans. Singer's clarion call is credited with arousing activists to take a stand, in effect creating the modern animal rights movement.

The message that much of animal research was inhumane and wasteful influenced large sections of the public. To the converts, cats and dogs are pets, not research animals, and monkeys are too uncomfortably close to humans to be the subjects of painful experiments. Perhaps more importantly, though, Singer's message (with public endorsement) garnered the attention of the scientists involved in animal research. With mounting public pressure and Singer's direct challenge to their ethics, scientists began to examine both the necessity of and the amount of cruelty involved in animal experimentation.

Agreement on the need for reform

Whether enlightened or simply bowing to public pressure, most animal researchers began to adhere to the principle of the "three Rs": replacement, reduction, and refinement. First advocated in 1959 by British scientists William M.S. Russell and Rex L. Burch, the three Rs call for replacing animal experiments with alternative methods, reducing the number of animals used in specific experiments, and refining the experiments to eliminate unnecessary suffering. By focusing on the three Rs and other principles of reform, animal researchers changed their procedures in two important ways. First, greater emphasis was placed on finding and utilizing alternative methods of research, and second, the number of large mammals used in research radically decreased. According to the National Survey of Laboratory Animal Facilities and Resources, the number of animals used in research dropped 40 percent between 1968 and 1978. Of this the greatest decline occurred in the use of cats and dogs. By 1997 cats and dogs made up less than 1 percent of the estimated 17 to 22 million animals used in research in the United States; nonhuman primates made up .3 percent of the total; and rats, mice, and other rodents accounted for roughly 90 percent.

Disagreement in ethics and practice

The marked decrease in animal experimentation, however, has not pacified those who oppose the practice. For many, the objection is moral: Animal experimentation is the cruel use of another sentient being for human gain. Others attest that it is poor science to believe that the results of animal experimentation can be applied to humans. Practicing physicians Neal D. Barnard and Stephen R. Kaufman state that the uniqueness of animal physiologies introduces an uncertainty into experiments that "severely undermines the extrapolation of animal data to other species, including humans." Still others such as Marc Bekoff, a biology professor at Colorado University, believe that animal tests are outdated: "People are wrong to think that everyone who advocates non-animal alternatives are doing it only because of the moral issues. Ultimately, better biomedical science will be forthcoming when people pay attention to alternatives."

Alternatives to animal experimentation are becoming more common. In medical research and product testing, computer models, tissue cultures, and synthetic skins have replaced animal specimens. But many researchers believe that there is simply no substitute for the information gleaned from testing on live subjects. For them, computer models and the like cannot predict how experimental drugs, for example, will react with complex bodily systems. Thus, the practical means of research defines the morality of using animals for some scientists. Other advocates of animal experimentation believe the end results justify their moral position. Richard Jones, another biology professor at Colorado University, insists, "Nobody that I know of, in biological research, who has to sacrifice animals, likes it. It's a matter of priorities. You do what the greater good is." These scientists point to past medical breakthroughs that involved animal testing and claim that such improvements in human health warrant the sacrifice.

No prospect of compromise

The debate over animal experimentation continues to pervade both the realms of medical practice and medical ethics, as well as other fields that range from military to commercial to educational. The two sides of the controversy agree on the need to reduce both the number of animals used in experiments and the amount of pain the animals experience, but they differ most vehemently on the feasibility of eliminating animal experimentation altogether. One side maintains that human welfare necessitates animal sacrifice, while the other side insists that human society cannot morally endorse speciesism. In a 1997 issue of *Scientific American*, staff writer Madhusree Mukerjee lays out a deceptively simple resolution to the debate:

> Animal liberators need to accept that animal research is beneficial to humans. And animal researchers need to admit that if animals are close enough to humans that their bodies, brains and even psyches are good models for the human condition, then ethical dilemmas surely arise in using them.

With strongly held opinions on both sides, such a moral compromise seems unattainable. The viewpoints in *At Issue: Animal Experimentation* attest to the fact that, although the use of animals in experiments has noticeably declined since 1975, the controversy surrounding the practice has not.

1

Animal Research Saves Human Lives

Heloisa Sabin

Heloisa Sabin is the honorary director of Americans for Medical Progress, an organization that believes animal experimentation is necessary for medical research. She is also the widow of Albert Sabin, the scientist who developed a polio vaccine in 1957.

While perfecting his vaccine against polio, Albert Sabin conducted tests on many animals. The sacrifice of these animals has enabled entire generations of humans to grow up without fear of the crippling effects of polio. Animal rights advocates who see animal experimentation as cruel and wasteful overlook the fact that it has been instrumental in developing medicines that have saved countless human lives.

That scene in "Forrest Gump," in which young Forrest runs from his schoolmate tormentors so fast that his leg braces fly apart and his strong legs carry him to safety may be the only image of the polio epidemic of the 1950s etched in the minds of those too young to remember the actual devastation the disease caused. Hollywood created a scene of triumph far removed from the reality of the disease.

Some who have benefited directly from polio research, including the work of my late husband, Albert Sabin, think winning the real war denounces the very process that enables them to look forward to continued good health and promising futures. This "animal rights" ideology—espoused by groups such as People for the Ethical Treatment of Animals, the Humane Society of the U.S. and the Fund for Animals—rejects the use of laboratory animals in medical research and denies the role such research played in the victory over polio.

The leaders of this movement seem to have forgotten that year after year in the early '50s, the very words "infantile paralysis" and "poliomyelitis" struck great fear among young parents that the disease would snatch their children as they slept. Each summer public beaches, playgrounds and movie theaters were places to be avoided. Polio epidemics condemned millions of children and young adults to lives in which debilitated lungs could no longer breathe on their own and young limbs were left forever wilted and frail. The disease drafted tiny armies of children on crutches and in wheelchairs who were unable to walk, run or jump. In the U.S., polio struck down nearly 58,000 children in 1952 alone.

Unlike the braces on Forrest Gump's legs, real ones would be replaced only as the children's misshapened legs grew. Other children and young adults were entombed in iron lungs. The only view of the world these patients had was through mirrors over their heads. These, however, are no longer part of our collective cultural memory.

Albert was on the front line of polio research. In 1961, thirty years after he began studying polio, his oral vaccine was introduced in the U.S. and distributed widely. In the nearly 40 years since, polio has been eradicated in the Western hemisphere, the World Health Organization reports, adding that with a full-scale effort, polio could be eliminated from the rest of the world by the year 2000.

Without animal research, polio would still be claiming thousands of lives each year. "There could have been no oral polio vaccine without the use of innumerable animals, a very large number of animals," Albert told a reporter shortly before his death in 1993. Animals are still needed to test every new batch of vaccine that is produced for today's children.

Without animal research, polio would still be claiming thousands of lives each year.

Animal activists claim that vaccines really didn't end the epidemics—that, with improvements in social hygiene, polio was dying out anyway, before the vaccines were developed. This is untrue. In fact, advanced sanitation was responsible in part for the dramatic rise in the number of paralytic polio cases in the '50s. Improvements in sanitation practices reduced the rate of infection, so that the average age of those infected by the polio virus went up. Older children and young adults were more likely than infants to develop paralysis from their exposure to the polio virus.

Every child who has tasted the sweet sugar cube or received the drops containing the Sabin Vaccine over the past four decades knows polio only as a word, or an obscure reference in a popular film. Thank heavens it's not part of their reality.

These polio-free generations have grown up to be doctors, teachers, business leaders, government officials, and parents. They have their own concerns and struggles. Cancer, heart disease, strokes and AIDS are far more lethal realities to them now than polio. Yet, those who support an "animal rights" agenda that would cripple research and halt medical science in its tracks are slamming the door on the possibilities of new treatments and cures.

My husband was a kind man, but he was impatient with those who refused to acknowledge reality or to seek reasoned answers to the questions of life.

The pioneers of polio research included not only the scientists but also the laboratory animals that played a critical role in bringing about the end of polio and a host of other diseases, for which we now have vaccines and cures. Animals will continue to be as vital as the scientists who study them in the battle to eliminate pain, suffering and disease from our lives.

That is the reality of medical progress.

2

Animal Experimentation Benefits AIDS Research

Joseph E. Murray

Dr. Joseph E. Murray, a Nobel laureate, performed the first human kidney transplant in 1954. He is a member of the board of directors of Americans for Medical Progress, an organization that believes animal experimentation is necessary for medical research.

In December 1995, AIDS patient Jeff Getty underwent an experimental treatment that involved injecting bone marrow cells from a baboon into his body to bolster his immune system (baboons are immune to the AIDS virus). The loss of the donor baboon was tolerable because scientists and doctors should use all methods at hand when combating deadly human diseases. Like the many other treatments and medicines that have contributed to improved human health, the cure for AIDS will undoubtedly come through animal experimentation. (Editor's note: Getty's body rejected the baboon cells, but he continues to look for other cures.)

The recent experimental transplant of bone marrow cells from a baboon into a human AIDS patient has already elicited one conclusion: Americans must decide whether they support animal research or "animal rights."

Even before Jeff Getty entered San Francisco General Hospital for the procedure, the public relations machinery of PETA, the Humane Society of the United States and other groups that take the extreme animal rights view went into high gear with the message that humans have no right to interfere with animals, even if lives are in the balance—which they are; AIDS research would be impossible without animal experimentation.

Animal activists, in commentaries, letters to the editor and TV news sound bites, have blasted researchers' latest attempt to find an effective treatment for AIDS. This offensive against scientific inquiry comes as no surprise. In 1990, PETA's founder, Ingrid Newkirk, told a magazine reporter that if animal research resulted in a cure for AIDS, "we'd be against it."

Reprinted from Joseph E. Murray, "Animals Hold the Key to Saving Human Lives," *Los Angeles Times*, February 5, 1996, by permission of the author.

Animal activists oppose all animal-based medical research. If we had listened to their arguments 50 years ago, children still would be contracting polio (the vaccine was developed in monkeys). Diabetics would not have insulin, a benefit of research on dogs. We would also be without antibiotics for pneumonia, chemotherapy for cancer, surgery for heart diseases, organ transplants and joint replacement.

Today, once again, the animal activists are wrong. And we can't let a potential treatment for AIDS fall victim to their specious rhetoric.

This debate is not just about AIDS and Jeff Getty's immune system. The knowledge gained from this experiment could have an impact on cancer therapy. The research almost certainly will enable doctors someday to treat leukemia, aplastic anemia and lymphoma patients with human bone marrow that is less than a perfect match and to open the pool of potential organ donors to include animals.

Finding a cure warrants the sacrifice

There are honest differences of opinion in the scientific community about the assumptions on which the Getty experiment is based. Although I am not directly involved in this research, I am convinced that all reasonable approaches must be objectively investigated if we are to conquer AIDS.

Animal activists condemn the experiment as morally wrong because the baboon donor was killed. In practical terms, they say, even if the transplant works, there are not enough baboons to provide marrow cells for all AIDS patients.

The baboon donor for the Getty experiment, raised in captivity for research,was fully anesthetized while the marrow cells were drawn. The animal was sacrificed then because all tissues had to be preserved for further scientific study. In the future, when the procedure moves out of the experimental phase, scientists will be able to harvest the necessary cells without sacrificing an animal. Ultimately, sufficient numbers of cells will almost certainly be grown in cultures. As has been the case in countless other medical treatments, the initial techniques will be simplified as the procedure becomes more routine.

For all its potential, there are no guarantees that the procedure will work, that the transplanted cells will take hold in Getty's system or that they will provide him with any increased immunity. Nor are there any guarantees that he will be safe from baboon diseases. Guarantees are not the nature of medical research.

Scientists agree that whenever a cure for AIDS is found, it will be through animal research.

Medical research is a lengthy, highly risky and expensive process with no certainties. Without taking the time, braving the risks and paying the costs, there can be no success. The Getty experiment is an important step in this ongoing process. Scientists agree that whenever a cure for AIDS is found, it will be through animal research.

Medical researchers are working for the health of us all. They should not be diverted from that essential purpose by irrational "animal rights" demands. Lies, threats, intimidation and violence by the movement's extremists already have delayed scientists' projects and delayed the benefits of their research from reaching the public.

As we approach the 15th anniversary of the discovery of the AIDS virus, it is not enough to wear red ribbons and hope that a cure is found. We must actively support those scientists, doctors and brave volunteers such as Jeff Getty who are on the front lines of research.

3

Animal Research Has Led to Medical Breakthroughs

Seriously Ill for Medical Research

Seriously Ill for Medical Research (SIMR) is an independent, voluntary patients' group formed to voice support for humane research into disabling, incurable, and progressive diseases. The organization is based in Britain.

Despite the inflammatory rhetoric of animal rights' spokespeople, the benefits of animal experimentation to humans and other animals outweigh the costs in terms of the number of animals used in research. The information garnered from experimenting on these animals has proved invaluable in treating and curing human ailments. From developing vaccines to treating Alzheimer's disease, animal research has aided doctors in countering numerous illnesses.

We are fortunate to live in a time when we no longer have to fear the many common diseases which were the main causes of childhood death only a century ago. These diseases have been conquered by medical research. Despite the enormous medical advances of the last 100 years, there are still many serious illnesses for which no effective treatment is known, from cystic fibrosis to Alzheimer's disease. Continuing medical research is the hope for future generations. A great many medical breakthroughs have depended on the use of laboratory animals and much of the medical research being done today still depends on them. Yet this research faces increasingly hostile campaigns by those who, through lack of understanding, would seek to ban all animal research. It is very important that we examine the facts.

For every £1 spent on medical research, only 5p [5 percent of £1] is spent on animal experiments, which are vital and complement computer studies, test tube experiments and studying people. If we look at the number of laboratory animals used, and the potential improvements in quality of life for both humans and other animals arising from such research, then we can see that the benefits far outweigh the costs. The following facts bring animal experimentation into a realistic focus:

- It is estimated that 2 million cats and dogs are abandoned as unwanted pets every year, and even more animals are destroyed as vermin. The RSPCA alone has to handle 2,000 cats and dogs every day.
- Last year 500 million animals were slaughtered for human consumption but less than 3 million animals were used in medical research. That's roughly equivalent to one mouse per person every 20 years.
- Of all the areas of animal use, including agriculture, pets, sports and animal research, the standards of welfare and veterinary care laid down are the highest for animals kept in laboratories for research.

In this article we detail the role played—and still being played—by animal research in the development of treatments for a range of diseases.

Vaccines and viral infections

Human viral diseases include the common cold, influenza, and more recently AIDS. Other viral diseases like smallpox, polio, mumps and measles are preventable due to vaccines developed with animal experiments. Viruses can invade many parts of the body, causing serious harm to vital organs such as kidney, liver or brain. The emergence of AIDS illustrates the constant and urgent need for ways of combatting new viral infections. In Britain about 16,000 people are HIV positive. Several animal species are infected by similar immuno-deficiency viruses and the study of these is vital to the understanding of HIV and AIDS that will lead to effective treatments or vaccines. Already more than 150 drugs exist or are under development and 13 potential vaccines are being developed. The current aim is to stop the virus multiplying and hopefully disarm it without harming the host cells.

A great many medical breakthroughs have depended on the use of laboratory animals and much of the medical research being done today still depends on them.

Since 1978, not a single person in the world has caught smallpox. That's because almost everyone was vaccinated against it. Now that smallpox has disappeared children today don't need to be vaccinated against it. The vaccine had to be obtained from calves and was tested on animals to make sure it was safe.

Before children were given polio vaccinations about 30,000 children in North America and Europe caught polio every year. There are about a million people alive today who would have caught polio if they had not been vaccinated. The vaccine was developed using animals in the 1950s and then finally tested on monkeys, to make sure it was effective and safe.

Vaccines for immunisation against the six most common childhood diseases—measles, diphtheria, whooping cough, tetanus, polio and tuberculosis—are saving the lives of over 3 million children every year, or six every minute, says UNICEF. In 1990 more than 100 million children under the age of one year were successfully immunised, and the UN Secretary General announced that eight out of every ten of the world's children are now immunised. That still leaves 2 million children who die each year because they are not immunised. A target of immunising 9 out of every 10 children throughout the world has been set for the year 2000.

Antibiotics and bacterial infections

Bacterial infection occurs when harmful bacteria enter the body and avoid destruction by the body's defense system. Examples of bacterial infection are pneumonia, typhoid, cholera, scarlet fever and legionnaires disease. Antibiotics have revolutionized the treatment of these life threatening conditions and now they can be treated with a good rate of recovery. The introduction of the first antibiotic, penicillin, in 1941, saved millions of lives. Animals have played an important role in our understanding of bacterial disease and in developing antibiotics.

Nowadays, potential new antibiotics are investigated initially in testtubes. But they must be evaluated for safety and effectiveness in animals before being tested and used in people.

Cancer

In Britain, 440 people die from cancer every day; three of them will be children under 15.

However two main advances have increased chances of survival. One of the first breakthroughs was the development of radiotherapy, in which radiation kills the tumour without causing too much damage to the rest of the body. Then came chemotherapy—drugs that kill the rapidly dividing cancer cells. Both of these techniques were developed and tested with the help of animal experiments.

For the 700 or so people in the UK this year who will develop a type of cancer called Hodgkin's disease, the advances in treatment mean that 500 of them will still be alive in five years. Without any treatment people with Hodgkin's disease always die. Similar progress has occurred in other cancer studies. Today 6 out of every 10 children with leukaemia can be cured. Overall 4 out of 10 people who develop cancer are now cured. Twenty years ago, the figure was 2 out of 10. Further effective research means more people being successfully treated.

Genetic diseases

The recent intensification of research in the field of genetic diseases will open the door to finding treatments for a wide range of disorders, not just the obviously inherited ones but also those thought to have a genetic background, e.g., diabetes, cardiovascular disease, common cancers, the major mental illnesses and many more. The diseases known to be caused by a single gene defeat will probably be tackled first. Since these affect one in every hundred infants born, that alone is a massive task.

Work on the mouse has made major contributions to knowledge of human genetics. The genetic constitution of mouse and man are surprisingly similar. The recently developed technique of trans-genesis, which enables, for example, a disease-causing human gene mutation to be replicated in a mouse, or a normal human gene to be placed in a diseased animal, is opening new horizons in the study of inherited diseases. It is remarkable that, over a period of less than ten years, the genes responsible for nearly all the relatively common inherited diseases have been located, and many of them have been isolated by cloning. For example, Duchenne muscular dystrophy, cystic fibrosis, haemophilia, neurofibromatosis, Huntingdon's disease, infantile spinal muscular atrophy and many others. Genetic research, using mostly the mouse, is set to revolutionise our medical understanding and gives hope of finding cures where previous hope did not exist.

Animals have played an important role in our understanding of bacterial disease and in developing antibiotics.

Two male children are born with Duchenne muscular dystrophy every week in Britain. Their muscle cells lack an essential substance so they gradually develop muscular weakness in infancy and will probably die in their mid-20s. The exact genetic abnormality found in sufferers is also found in some mice, and research using these mice is providing valuable clues to the condition and to potential treatments.

At present the life expectancy of cystic fibrosis is only slightly better, and it affects 1 in 2,000 children. CF robs victims of lung, heart and pancreas functions, and often triggers pneumonia. At the moment, heart-lung transplants offer the only hope of long-term survival.

Recent reports of successful gene therapy in mice may lead to simple, more effective treatment in [the] future.

Haemoglobin abnormalities cause potentially fatal anaemia, as the red blood cells cannot deliver enough oxygen to different parts of the body. They are the most common inherited disorders caused by a single gene defect. By the year 2000 it has been estimated that seven people in every hundred will be carriers of the two important haemoglobin disorders, sickle cell anaemia and thalassaemia. Although these diseases are relatively uncommon in this country, they are a major public health problem in other parts of the world as they affect people of Mediterranean, African and Asian descent. At present, the only satisfactory treatment is repeated transfusions, although the diseases can be prevented by carrier detection and prenatal diagnosis. The recent development, by genetic engineering, of a mouse model of sickle cell disease should enable doctors to understand why the red blood cells become deformed and to develop new approaches to treatment.

Autoimmune disorders

Several serious disorders are the result, either wholly or partially, of the defences of the body turning on themselves. These disorders have proved particularly difficult to understand and treat. With the help of animal models, doctors are now making progress on many fronts.

Rheumatic disease is the biggest single cause of disablement, and it can affect the whole of people's lives: even maintaining independence can be an anxious and continual battle. There are as many as 200 different kinds of rheumatic disease: the better known ones being rheumatoid arthritis (with a million sufferers in the UK), osteoarthritis (with 5–10 million sufferers), gout and ankylosing spondylitis. Great advances have been made, although there is as yet no cure for rheumatic disease.

Research is aimed at different aspects of the problem; understanding the causes and mechanisms of the disease, new surgical techniques, new materials for replacing affected joints (there are about 40,000 hip replacements every year in the UK) and new medicines to control and alleviate symptoms. Rats, rabbits and guinea pigs have been used to increase understanding of rheumatic disease.

Recent reports of successful gene therapy in mice may lead to simple, more effective treatment in [the] future.

Multiple sclerosis (MS) is a disease of the central nervous system that strips the protective myelin insulation from nerves within the body. This causes deterioration of body functions, such as muscle movement, balance, strength, speech and vision. It is estimated that about 80,000 people have MS in Britain.

Researchers have learned a lot about MS through a disease called experimental autoimmune encephalomyelitis. This laboratory induced disease, very similar to MS, occurs in rats, mice and guinea pigs. Using these animal models, researchers have studied the basic biological problems related to MS, and have shown that it may be possible to 'switch off' the disease by treatment with antibodies, and to transplant myelin-making cells, which can repair damaged nerves. These models have also been used to test whether potential MS drugs are effective and safe.

Diabetes is thought to be caused by a number of different factors—environmental, genetic and autoimmune. Seventy years ago, to be diagnosed diabetic was a death sentence. If you were young, you probably had less than a year to live. It is estimated that over 10 million diabetes sufferers have been saved from death since insulin was introduced. Today, in Britain alone, there are 600,000 people with diagnosed diabetes, of whom about 200,000 are insulin dependent. Another 600,000 people don't yet know they're diabetic. In diabetes, the pancreas cannot produce its own insulin, the hormone that enables the body to use sugar.

Insulin was first isolated from the pancreas of dogs by Frederick Banting and Charles Best at the University of Toronto in 1921. Insulin is a protein found in all animals, and, up until recently, diabetics used insulin produced from the cow and pig pancreas. It is purified, and then standardized by testing in mice. For each animal used, enough insulin is produced to treat 70 diabetics for a year. Insulin saves lives, every day, by controlling diabetes and enabling people to live more or less normally. But it is a treatment, not a cure.

Research continues, using mouse and rat models, with the aim of finding safe and effective treatments which do not require daily injections. Ultimately, the aim of the research is to find a prevention or cure: current studies indicate that transplants of insulin producing cells from animals may be possible in the future.

Heart disease

Coronary heart disease is a major cause of suffering and premature death. It kills 1 person in 4 in Western societies despite significant advances in treatment over the last 30 years or so. The development of the heart-lung machine in the 1940s made open heart surgery possible. About a third of a million pacemakers are implanted annually worldwide to regulate faltering heart beats, and in this country about 6,000 operations are carried out every year to repair or replace faulty heart valves. In the 1960s a major new surgical technique was developed to by-pass damaged arteries and some 13,000 coronary by-pass operations are now performed in Britain every year. More recently, heart transplants have enabled some patients to enjoy many more years of active life: about 450 are carried out every year, with a 90% success rate. This is helped by immunosuppressive drugs which are used to prevent rejection after all organ transplant operations. Beta-blocking drugs to reduce high blood pressure and prevent heart attacks were developed in the late 1950s. Animal research was essential in the development of all these treatments.

Tropical diseases

Thanks to vaccines and antibiotics, infectious diseases are no longer life threatening, in the UK at least. But in the third world, parasitic disease is still a major killer. Malaria has increased dramatically in recent years. Nearly 300 million people are infected with malaria and 2 million die every year. Treatment and control are difficult because of drug-resistant strains of malaria and insecticide-resistant strains of mosquito. Finding a vaccine is the top priority but potential vaccines must be safe. Animal tests are the vital link between the test-tube and people in this research.

Kidney disease

Over 3,000 people a year in the UK develop kidney failure. A third of these would die without regular dialysis on a kidney machine, or a kidney transplant.

The kidney machine, which removes toxic waste products from the blood, was a direct result of work on rabbits and dogs. It is vital during dialysis to prevent the blood clotting as it passes through the machine, and this is achieved by adding the drug heparin. The anti-clotting action of heparin was discovered by experiments in dogs, and today the drug is obtained from beef liver.

Transplant surgery often offers the only real hope for kidney patients, and over 20,000 successful kidney transplants have been carried out in the UK since the technique was first developed using dogs in the 1950s. Again, anti-rejection drugs, developed by testing their ability to prevent rejection of grafts in mice, are vital to the survival of the transplanted organ. Now, nearly 2,000 kidney transplants are performed every year in Britain.

Asthma

More than two million people suffer from asthma in Britain. It affects 1 in every 10 children though many cases are not being properly diagnosed. Severe asthma causes tremendous suffering and can be lethal; last year it killed 2,000.

There are drugs which relieve the symptoms of asthma, but do little to prevent the underlying worsening of the disease. New drugs will require very thorough development, refinement and research on animals for both effectiveness and safety. Animal research is continuing to improve our understanding of asthma and its treatment.

Alzheimer's disease

Alzheimer's disease is a progressive brain disorder affecting about 500,000 people in Britain. It is very disturbing to see the elderly, and sometimes the not so elderly, suffering from almost complete memory loss, a symptom of this illness. Research on mice has already demonstrated that abnormalities (structures called plaques) seen in the brains of Alzheimer's patients are due to the formation of a particular protein. This mouse model of Alzheimer's disease, produced by genetic engineering, will prove invaluable in developing ways of treating or preventing the disease.

Epilepsy

Most people have heard of epilepsy. This unpredictable condition afflicts about 300,000 men, women and children in Britain: that's about 1 in every 200 people. Today's medicines offer several effective treatments. Usually just one medicine is sufficient, but sometimes a combination has to be used. Even so, in 1 in 5 cases, no treatment seems to work. This means that around 60,000 people in Britain alone face the possibility of a sudden attack at any time with no means of alleviating it. Research into understanding the function of the brain and the changes which occur during epileptic seizures must go on, if new anti-epileptic medicines are to be discovered. Much of what is known today about epilepsy has been gained by studying animals, particularly the mouse.

Veterinary medicine

The tremendous benefit that all animals receive from veterinary research is often overlooked, not just for our pets but also for farm animals. Dogs in particular suffer from a variety of diseases: distemper, infectious hepatitis, leptospirosis, kennel cough and parvovirus infection can be controlled by vaccines which were all developed with animal experiments. A typical example of the efficiency of such research is that for each laboratory animal used in the research, 75,000 dogs can now be protected for life against distemper. Cats suffer from cat flu, feline enteritis and leukaemia, all of which can be prevented by vaccinations. Many of the medicines used to treat animals—antibiotics, pain killers, anaesthetics, tranquilisers—are exactly the same as those used to treat people.

The voice of the sufferers

These examples should make it perfectly clear to everyone just how much we owe to the use of animals in medical research. Not only for past and present treatments but also for future research to conquer currently incurable illnesses.

SIMR is an independent, voluntary organisation formed to promote research into crippling, debilitating and progressive diseases and to support the humane use of animals in medical research. SIMR is the voice of the sufferers, the people who actually have the highest stakes at risk—their lives.

If you would like to support SIMR, why not join us today?

4

The Animal Rights Movement Slows Medical Progress

Susan E. Paris

Susan E. Paris is former president of Americans for Medical Progress (AMP) Educational Foundation, a nonprofit organization that is dedicated to informing the public, the media, and policy makers about biomedical research. AMP is based in Alexandria, Virginia.

Perhaps the most overlooked threat to medical science is the animal rights movement. Those who wish to save the lives of research animals and sacrifice the welfare of patients who benefit from animal experimentation are wrongheaded and dangerous. The animal rights movement has been effective in getting regulations passed that hamper medical research, and their terrorist tactics of setting lab animals free or firebombing research facilities have resulted in millions of dollars in damages. These extremist measures are endangering the lives of those waiting for cures acquired through animal research.

Owing to the ongoing debate over health-care reform, we've all become conversant on such once-esoteric subjects as "managed care" and "universal coverage." We're all interested in the matter, and the fact that politicians are meeting the issue head-on illustrates the power of public pressure.

But there is one threat to human health that has slipped through a loophole in the public consciousness. It is a threat that has the potential to slow medical progress to a tedious crawl, delaying and sometimes stopping the search for cures and treatments.

This threat takes the form of an anti–medical research movement, better known as animal rights. And because the public has failed to expose the movement's agenda and to condemn its tactics, it is growing stronger, more destructive, and more difficult to stop.

Reprinted from Susan E. Paris, "Animal Rights Advocates' Actions Pose Big Threat to Public Health," *The Scientist*, vol. 8, no. 17, September 5, 1994, with permission.

This is no longer a movement composed of a small band of extremists. Membership in animal rights groups has grown fivefold since 1984, making it one of the fastest-growing social movements in the United States today. Further, letters concerning animals now constitute the third largest volume of mail to the U.S. Congress, exceeded only by those concerned with Social Security and the federal deficit. The animal rightists have also got the support of Hollywood's wealthy elite. Noted celebrities Kim Basinger, Alec Baldwin, and Paul and Linda McCartney, for example, all wave the animal rights banner for People for the Ethical Treatment of Animals (PETA), the largest animal rights group in the U.S. This widespread support has been achieved through a tremendous public manipulation campaign.

The radical aims of the animal rights movement

Like many extremist groups, the animal rights movement cloaks its radical intentions under the guise of compassion, hoodwinking the public into believing animal extremists wish to strike a balance between human and animal interests.

Yet, unlike the concept of animal welfare, which we all support, the animal-rights agenda calls for a fundamental change in the relationship between humans and animals—from one of responsible stewardship to one of absolute equality.

Chief among the animal rights movement's goals is to abolish all medical research work with animals, no matter how necessary or humane. Ingrid Newkirk, cofounder and president of PETA, has stated publicly: "Animal research is immoral, even if it is essential."

Of course, you won't find this statement in PETA's direct-mail fundraising letters, or in its public presentations. But every single dollar of the $10 million donated annually to PETA fuels the spread of this philosophy. The same is true for the other $190 million donated to other animal rights groups nationwide.

The animal rights movement uses a classic extremist strategy. The political wing presses forward on the propaganda front while the covert wing plants the bombs.

Chief among the animal rights movement's goals is to abolish all medical research work with animals, no matter how necessary or humane.

Animal-rights lobbyists have had great success stopping medical research with legislative red tape and regulation. They have helped shift billions of dollars in medical-research funds into compliance with excessive regulations that do not contribute to the welfare of animals, but simply waste scarce resources.

For example, laboratories, zoos, animal dealers, and auction operators spent an estimated $2 billion in 1990 complying with tougher federal rules covering the housing, feeding, watering, sanitation, and ventilation of animals.

Terrorist methods and the toll on research

Those extremists for whom the legislative process moves too slowly resort to more dangerous tactics. The Department of Justice issued a report to Congress in September 1993 that documented 313 instances of animal-rights terrorism in the U.S. since 1977, causing an estimated $1.37 million in direct damages. According to the report, security costs for animal enterprises have risen anywhere from 10 percent to 20 percent as a result of extremist animal-rights activity. Bulletproof glass had to be installed in the windows of the laboratory animal-care facility at the University of California, Berkeley. The cost of this security measure was $55,000.

It is impossible to account for the costs in terms of human suffering and loss as a result of delayed or aborted research. But it is easy to see how the hopes of those in need of cures and treatments are left in a pile of debris with the torched remains of our nation's research enterprises.

Americans recognize a need to deal with the health-care crisis. We have seen the problematic signs—rising costs of care and Americans without coverage—and we have acted. But all of the work being put into improving our health-care system will be for naught if we allow a powerful band of self-righteous activists to deny us the privilege of studying non-human animals—medical science's most valuable tool in the fight against disease.

5

The World's Major Religions Condone Animal Experimentation

Seriously Ill for Medical Research

Seriously Ill for Medical Research (SIMR) is an independent, voluntary patients' group formed to voice support for humane research into disabling, incurable, and progressive diseases. The organization is based in Britain.

The use of animals in medical research is, in part, a moral concern. Representatives of the major religions of the world have issued statements regarding the morality of sacrificing animals for human welfare. All agree that human life is more valuable than animal life, and therefore condone animal experimentation for human benefit. Scientists concerned about the morality of their experiments and animal activists who would decry such research on moral grounds should recognize that the world's major religions all believe animal experimentation to be morally acceptable.

The use of animals for medical research is a complex scientific and moral issue. It is easy to point to the scientific and medical benefits that have been gained using animals, but this does not resolve the unease that many people and researchers feel about whether it is morally right to take the life of animals in pursuit of scientific knowledge and better medical treatments. Many people gain their moral values from the organised religions and even secular people would find it impossible to deny the importance of religion to the social and political lives of most countries.

Sometimes a religious standpoint is clearly given in the holy books, sometimes an interpretation or official pronouncement is made by a religious leader based on a written passage. It is noteworthy that, while all religions recognise the importance of animals in the world, none of the world's major religions holds ceremonies to mark the birth or death of animals. This point emphasises the relative importance placed on animal life compared to human life by the major religions. Nonetheless, the morality of the use of animals is an important issue, and the world's reli-

Reprinted, with permission, from "The Major Religions on Animals and Medical Research," an electronic article from the website of the Seriously Ill for Medical Research: www.simr.dircon.co.uk/religion.html.

gions consider that it lies properly within their domain.

> The views of the world's great religions on the use of animal experimentation for scientific purposes need to be brought to the attention of both scientists and animal protection groups.[1]

Broadly, the major religions all propose the following points:
- That human life is more valuable than animal life. From the religious perspective this is based on the belief that humans are uniquely responsible and capable of salvation. This is quite different from the philosophical view that human life is more valuable because humans are more aware of pain and pleasure.
- That humans have a God-given authority over other animals. Usually expressed as 'dominion' or 'stewardship,' it implies a position of trust and also responsibility.
- It is recognised that humans eat animals and use them for other reasons such as work. The right to do these things is enshrined in most religions.
- That cruelty to animals is to be abhorred because it displays attributes that are undesirable in civilised societies. By this is meant pointless acts that will cause an animal to experience pain or suffering.
- Besides the previous point which condemns cruelty, most religions positively urge kindness towards animals.

Protestant Christianity

Church of England. A key reference in the New Testament on this topic is *Matthew 10 vv. 29–31.* All the Christian denominations take this as a starting point.

> A man is worth many sparrows, but not one sparrow can die unnoticed in God's World.

The Church of England has specifically made statements about the relationships between humankind and animals. Mostly these predate the 1986 Animals (Scientific Procedures) Act and arose from consultation between the church and the government.

> The fact that animals may be used in scientific procedures for the benefit of people shows that we believe that human beings have more value than animals. But the fact that we minimise the pain, suffering, distress or lasting harm that animals may have to undergo shows that we regard them as having intrinsic value.[2]

Baptists. The Social Affairs office of the Baptist Church in a private communication says:

> [Most Baptists] would be sympathetic to the use of animals in medical research, but less enthusiastic about their use in cosmetic products.[3]

Methodism. The Methodist church has issued a statement on the subject of the treatment of animals.

It should be horrifying that millions of animals are killed every year in laboratory experiments, but most of them have been bred for the purpose and the outcome of the experimentation is valuable advance in both human and veterinary medicine.

Unnecessary or unjustifiable experimentation, as on the effect of cosmetics; the use of numbers of animals in an experiment far in excess of a reasonable control and check number; excessive duplication of experiments in different laboratories; the use of animals when valid results could be secured from tissue cultures; are all to be condemned.[4]

Some of these requirements are exactly those of the current controls on medical research involving animals in Britain. The Animals (Scientific Procedures) Act 1986 states, among other things, that all such procedures require a licence that provides evidence of the need to perform those procedures, and that no licence will be issued if there is any valid alternative to using animals.[5]

It is noteworthy that, while all religions recognise the importance of animals in the world, none of the world's major religions holds ceremonies to mark the birth or death of animals.

Quakers. There is no tradition of authoritative statements from the organising body of Quakers, according to Beth Smith, General Secretary of Quaker Social Responsibility and Education. She goes as far as to say:

The most controversial area of animal exploitation for Quakers is that of medical experimentation. There are many Quaker doctors and some medical researchers who hold Home Office licences to experiment on live animals. The latter would justify their actions by citing the beneficial results which they feel can be achieved for humans and animals through the knowledge gained.[6]

Quakers prefer to allow the individual members to come to their own conclusions about the morality of animal experimentation, but they are generally tolerant towards those individuals who do support it.

Catholicism

An interpretation of the Catholic Catechism is offered by Nicholas Coote, the Assistant General Secretary of the Catholic Bishops' Conference of England and Wales. He stresses that the Catechism should be seen only as a starting point for further discussion.

Provided they remain within reasonable limits, medical and scientific experiments on animals are morally acceptable since they may help to save human lives or advance therapy.[7]

At the Vth International Conference on the Brain and Mind, the Pope himself emphasised the importance of medical research to benefit humankind.

> My praise and encouragement, then, go out to all of you—scientists, doctors, researchers, scholars, and pastors of souls who devote yourselves with impassioned commitment to studying the very noble and profound subject of the human mind. . . . The boundless field of the neurosciences—from neurobiology to neurochemistry, from psychosomatic medicine to psychoendocrinology—offers research the possibility of approaching in a particularly penetrating way the threshold of the very mystery of man.[8]

Judaism

Judaism recognises that animal experimentation holds many benefits for humankind and animals.

> Isserles (Ramah) states that anything necessary for medical or other useful purposes is excluded from the prohibition of cruelty to animals.[9]

Rabbi John D Rayner, Chairman of the Council of Reform and Liberal Rabbis, offers this quotation from *What Does Judaism Say About . . . ?* by Rabbi Dr Peter Jacobs.

> A very good case can be made out for vivisection of animals provided safeguards are taken to reduce the pain to a minimum. Here the benefits to medical progress are considerable and the price worth paying.[10]

Rabbi Rayner himself adds:

> [I] would regard any experimentation on animals as ethically permissible provided (a) that it is done in such a way as to cause the least possible suffering to the animals and (b) that there is real basis for the hope that such experimentation may lead to the saving of human life or the relief of human suffering.
>
> Indeed, I would be inclined to add a further condition, namely that authority to permit such experimentation should be vested in an ethics committee composed of persons who have no interest in the potential commercial value of any pharmaceutical products that may be [the] result from such experimentation.[11]

The Animals (Scientific Procedures) Act requires that painkillers and anaesthetics are used whenever necessary, and that veterinary attention should be available to animals used in medical research. Furthermore, licences are granted (or refused) by Home Office Inspectors who have no commercial interest in the products of animal procedures. A separate advisory committee, the Animal Procedures Committee, advises the Home Secretary.

Islam

An interpretation of the statements about animals in the Qur'an is given by the author and Qur'anic scholar Al-Hafiz B A Masri:

> Some research on animals may yet be justified, given the traditions of Islam. Basic and applied research in the biological and social sciences, for example, will be allowed, if the laboratory animals are not caused pain or disfigured, and if human beings or other animals would benefit because of the research.

> Actions shall be judged according to intention. Any kind of medical treatment of animals and experiments on them becomes ethical and legal or unethical and illegal according to the intention of the person who does it.[12]

Hinduism and Sikhism

Hinduism and its close relative, Sikhism, are different from Judaism, Christianity or Islam in that they have no 'bible' or 'rule book' giving instruction. The sacred texts, for example, the Sri Isopanisad, require some interpretation by the reader or a priest. Any quotes from Hindu religious writings should be read with this in mind. There are many ways in which Hinduism or Sikhism may be practised and this can vary greatly between communities and individuals.

Provided they remain within reasonable limits medical and scientific experiments on animals are morally acceptable since they may help to save human lives or advance therapy.

There are central tenets to the Hindu faith, most notably the belief in reincarnation, sometimes as an animal. All animal life is revered because in the eyes of a Hindu all animals are the receptacles of souls. Consequently, Hindus have a general aim to be vegetarian, but many are not. There are also many Hindu doctors and medical researchers who use animals in research.

Any decision about the morality of animal experiments is left to the individual. While some followers of Hinduism would not choose to perform animal experiments, most would be tolerant of it because of its value to humans and animals.

One interpretation of the Sri Isopanisad is given by His Divine Grace A C Bhaktivedanta Swami Prabhupada, writing on the subject of animals:

> A human life is distinguished from animal life due to its heavy responsibilities. . . . The human being is given all facilities for a comfortable life by the laws of nature because the human form of life is more important and valuable than animal life. . . . As human beings we are not meant for sim-

ply solving economic problems on a tottering platform but for solving all the problems of the material life into which we have been placed by the laws of nature.[13]

This extract comments upon the burdens placed upon humankind by virtue of being different from animals. According to the text these differences impose a duty on humankind to solve all the problems of the material life. This must logically include curing diseases, those most material of problems, and presumably acknowledges any reasonable use of animals in this respect.

Buddhism

Buddhism draws largely from Hinduism. The most devout—Zen Buddhists—believe that all life is sacred. More ordinary Buddhists will probably admit the necessity of taking animal life under certain circumstanses. The Buddhist standpoint is embodied in the first Precept:

> I undertake the rule of training not to do any harm to any living (breathing) thing.

This precept implies something more than simply not harming living things. It includes actively helping people or animals suffering from misfortune or disease and this process may involve the use of animals. In a personal communication, Ronald C Maddox, General Secretary of The Buddhist Society, says:

> All of us, it has to be admitted, have probably benefitted in some measure from animal experiments and their suffering. Some Buddhists may up to a point be willing to accept this in the interests of humanity. Others may themselves reject this and be fully willing to forego any potential benefits.[14]

Concern and tolerance

All the world's major religions either actively support the use of animals in medical research, or they are tolerant towards those who conduct such research. Pronouncements about this subject are always accompanied by a long tradition of concern for animal welfare, or statements which make it clear that medical research must be conducted with a high degree of concern for the welfare of the animals.

Any kind of medical treatment of animals and experiments on them becomes ethical and legal or unethical and illegal according to the intention of the person who does it.

In Britain this is precisely the way animal research is conducted. The law insists that all such work is licenced, that the licences are awarded by an impartial body (the Home Office), that some analysis of the benefits to be gained is weighed against the cost in terms of animal lives and that there is a system of public accountability as shown by the annual publication of the statistics and the report of the Animal Procedures Committee.

References

1. Rosner F. *Modern Medicine and Jewish Ethics*. New York: Ktav Publishing House Inc., 1986:317–333.

2. *Our Responsibility for the Living Environment*. Great Britain: Church House Press, 1986:29–32.

3. Rev. Anne Wilkinson-Hayes. Personal communication. The Baptist Union of Great Britain, Social Affairs Office, 13th Feb, 1992.

4. A Methodist Statement on the Treatment of Animals. Great Britain, 1980:1–3

5. Guidance on the Operation of the Animals (Scientific Procedures) Act 1986. GB: HMSO, 1990.

6. Beth Smith, General Secretary, Quaker Social Responsibility and Education. Personal communication. 17th March 1992. Quoting: *What the Churches Say on Moral and Social Issues*. Great Britain: Christian Education Movement.

7. Nicholas Coote, Assistant General Secretary, Catholic Bishops' Conference of England and Wales. Personal communication. 9th March 1993. Quoting: *The Catechism of the Catholic Church of England*.

8. Dolentium Hominum. Vth International Conference of the Brain and Mind, p10.

9. Rosner F. *Modern Medicine and Jewish Ethics*. New York: Ktav Publishing House Inc., 1986:317–333.

10. Jacobs P. *What Does Judaism Say About . . . ?* Keter Publishing House Jerusalem Ltd. 1973:24–29.

11. Rabbi John Rayner, Chairman, Council of Reform and Liberal Rabbis. Personal communication. 15th March 1992.

12. Masri, B.A., Al-Hafiz. *Animals in Islam*. Great Britain: Athene Trust. 1989:17.

13. AC Bhaktivedanta Swami Prabhupada. *The Sri Isopanisad*. Bhaktivedanta Book Trust, 1974:15–16 and 108.

14. Ronald C Maddox, General Secretary, The Buddhist Society. Personal communication. 14th May 1992.

6

Animals, Vegetables and Minerals: I Love Animals, and Can Still Work with Them in a Research Laboratory

Jessica Symczyk

Jessica Symczyk is a lab technician for a pharmaceutical company. She is also a volunteer spokesperson for Americans for Medical Progress, an organization that believes animal experimentation is necessary for medical research.

Being an animal lover and a medical researcher who uses animals does not present a conflict of interests. Working inside an animal experimentation laboratory dispels mistaken notions that research animals are treated poorly. These animals live in clean, well-lit environments and they are respected by their handlers. Furthermore, the work that is derived from animal research is important to medical progress.

I've been a vegetarian (an ovo-lacto vegetarian to be exact) since I was 13 years old. I don't wear cosmetics. I won't buy or wear fur. I refuse to wear or use leather if at all possible. And, I absolutely love animals. I live with fish, a mouse, a pony, a horse, cats, and I'm looking for the perfect dog to complement my other companion animals. Oh, yes. I also love rats. I've had rats for pets. The last was a big black-and-white-hooded rat. I even nursed an abandoned baby mouse, whose eyes had not yet opened, until she reached adulthood.

So why am I working in a biomedical research lab that uses animals in its experiments? No, I am not an infiltrator from the so-called "animal rights" movement. I love what I do and I get angry when I hear the terrible things groups like People for the Ethical Treatment of Animals say about me and my colleagues and how we supposedly treat laboratory animals.

If you buy into the words of some animal-rightists, I am the last person you would expect to find working at an animal research lab. Well, not only are these groups wrong about me and my profession; they are also grossly mistaken about my colleagues, our work and the conditions under which we keep our animals.

The work we do with animals is crucial. It's important to me as a woman, as a human, and as an animal lover. Although most of my work involves rodents, two new studies I find pretty exciting involve dogs. In one, my dogs undergo a minor surgical procedure and take one pill a day of a promising drug that may regenerate bone in victims of osteoarthritis, a condition that cripples many elderly folks. In the second, we're investigating a drug that stimulates T-cell and white-blood-cell production, something of vital importance to AIDS patients.

Both would likely be condemned by the rightists as cruel and unnecessary. Let me tell you the extent of the "cruelty" my dogs undergo. In the first study, they play with a lab technician for an hour every day.

The other experiment requires that they drink a tiny amount of an extremely diluted drug, about a fifth of a teaspoonful, a day for eight days and have some blood drawn. When I draw blood, the dogs are happy to see me and they romp about like bouncy pups. Contrary to popular belief, all animals are not euthanized at the end of a study. Those that are receive the same treatment from a veterinarian that your pet would in a veterinary hospital.

How do I justify my profession in view of my beliefs? I want to dispel any idea that I do what I do for the money. I wanted to work with animals—horses actually—since I was old enough to think such thoughts. My first job out of high school was working for a wonderful and compassionate veterinarian for $4 an hour. Until then I had always imagined myself working on a farm where I could train and ride horses.

I guess you could say my desire to work with animals caused me to go back to school, where I earned a degree in equine veterinary science with a minor in animal science. I spent a few years as a vet tech in private practice taking care of sick animals, assisting with surgery, and dealing with the pet owners. From that experience I can honestly say at least 25 percent of pet owners should never be allowed near any animals. The stories I could tell about pet mistreatment are not fit for any ears.

Truthfully, I never considered working in a biomedical lab until a friend invited me to apply where he worked. I did not know what to expect. TV images of dark, dirty, water-dripping dungeons floated in and out of my imagination. I didn't really want to go, but I knew he was a good person and would not be associated with a bad place, so I applied. The moment I stepped into the lab was a real eye-opener. I was impressed with how clean, well-lit, and modern the facilities are. It is more like a human hospital. The monitoring equipment, the sterile technique used in the surgery area, the anesthetics and painkillers for post-operative recovery are identical to what you would find in most hospitals for humans.

The animals themselves are frisky, playful, and quite happy to see the animal techs, who play with them whenever they have a free moment. All the dogs have play toys. Do you know of any other hospital where the patient is held in a nurse's arms until he or she awakes and is steady enough to walk alone? That is part of what I do for every animal that requires surgery whether it's a rat, mouse, cat, or a dog.

What impressed me then, and still does now that I am a part of the team, is the absolute honor, respect, and devotion all of us have for the animals. Love for animals is the rule not the exception. The protective clothing worn by visitors to the lab is to protect the animals.

The work we do with animals is crucial. It's important to me as a woman, as a human, and as an animal lover.

I take my profession very seriously. And I get very angry when I hear people who don't know what they are talking about rant and rave about "torture" and duplication of tests. The research we do is essential to humans and animals. Test duplications are sometimes needed to show that the results of the first study aren't a fluke. Less than 5 percent of our studies require any pain relief at all. A full 95 percent are less painful than a visit to the doctor for you or me.

I've thought about the difference between animal welfare and animal rights. The whole issue of moral and ethical treatment of animals has been one that has shaped how I live my life. But there are some animal-rightists whose definitions and priorities are so extreme that they just don't apply. PETA, I've read, envisions a future that would not allow me to keep my pets. And it considers a rat the equal of a child, so deciding to save one or the other would be a flip of a coin. I cannot accept this. My love for animals matches anyone's, but there is no question as to who would come first.

Biomedical research has become my life. I know how researchers treat lab animals including mice and rats. I see how the work we are doing truly benefits everyone, including animals. Today, dogs and cats can enjoy a three to five-year increase in their life expectancies thanks to research and the vaccines and medicines we developed. I'm glad to be working with animals and other animal lovers to find ways to make life better for both.

7

Human Self-Interest Will Ensure That Animal Experimentation Continues

Trevor Philips

Trevor Philips is a columnist who wrote this article for the Independent, *a United Kingdom newspaper.*

Animal experimentation occurs in the medical field and the field
of product testing. In both instances, the animals are being used
as substitutes for humans who would have to suffer and potentially die in order to gather the information that is used to safe-
guard products or aid human health. It is unfortunate that many
animals are sacrificed in catering to human desires, but human
self-interest dictates that any method of preserving human life
will be chosen over a concern for animal welfare.

I s the fact that my octogenarian mother might have the pleasure of seeing her second great-grandchild with her own eyes more important
than the pain and distress caused by the experiments on animals that
could lead to a treatment that would save her sight? The cost isn't just financial; it involves the cruelty done to millions of albino rabbits who
have irritants deliberately dropped into their eyes as part of the research
that may allow the elderly to keep seeing just a little longer.

Today is World Lab Animal Day, and I want you to stand in front of
the mirror and say to yourself that the question doesn't matter. You'd like
to, wouldn't you? After all it's really up to boffins to tell us the best thing
to do here. As with many other key decisions of our time, BSE [Bovine
Spongiform Encephalopathy, a.k.a. Mad Cow Disease] for example, we
wave our hands despairingly at the men in white coats, and declare that
it's all too difficult for ordinary mortals to handle.

Well, it isn't. It's very simple really. You have to decide what matters
most. I will admit that it would not distress me for a second if I never saw
another snake, rat or mouse in my life. I dislike them and they me. But
even if you discount them, there are all sorts of animals used in scientific

Reprinted from Trevor Philips, "Sometimes It Is Right to Sacrifice Animals for Our Own Well-
Being," *The Independent*, April 25, 1998, by permission of *The Independent*.

experimentation, and many of them are of the cuddly variety—monkeys, dogs, cats, and of course sheep, such as Dolly, who famously was created in a laboratory.

There are 2.7 million animals used in laboratory work every year in the UK. In the US, more than five million animals die each year as a result of so-called "lethal dose" tests. Their deaths are not accidental. The lethal dose procedure was devised to determine what amount of a substance would kill a given percentage of a sample of animals. Thus the test which has been used for most of this century, the LD50, or lethal dose 50, simply continues feeding poison to animals until 50 per cent die. And, sadly, the animals do not simply lie down and pass quietly away. They die painfully and distressingly.

None of this is any fun for the laboratory workers. If they didn't have to do it, they wouldn't. Dozens of companies now contribute money to charities dedicated to finding alternatives to testing on animals. This is partly because they believe in the cause; but it is probably also due to the fact that increasingly, consumers are asking awkward questions about the products they are buying, and there is nothing more likely to turn off a British consumer than any hint of cruelty to animals.

The buyers of cosmetics are well aware of the history of animal testing in this field; sooner rather than later we can expect to see a more complete labelling of proprietary drugs, and I should not be surprised if one day all household products will be required to carry a disclaimer stating that they have not been tested on animals. That doesn't even touch the vast range of other products made by companies engaged in animal testing. For example, it surprised me to learn that the makers of Post-Its and of Parker pens are both accused by the American organisation People for the Ethical Treatment of Animals—by no means the most extreme around—of using animals in their research.

Which of us, told that our son or daughter has been diagnosed with cancer, would say "save the bunny rabbit, [damn] the child"?

So far, so noble. We can all agree that no living thing should be put through one nanosecond of distress in testing anything as repulsive as a cigarette or as trivial as cosmetic products. But what about granny's eyesight? And even if we don't regard perfume as necessary, what about makeup for people who suffer from severe disfigurement which, if not hidden, can end up blighting their lives? Would we deny someone with vitiligo—the condition said to afflict the singer Michael Jackson—the chance to use safe makeup rather than be hidden away at home because of the embarrassment of having blotchy skin?

There is little doubt that huge advances are being made in finding alternatives to animal testing. New techniques allow for testing on dead animals, or on tissue cultures; there are advances in the use of corneas from eye banks, and the ubiquitous computer model is now offering scientists a reliable tool for testing innovative products without using animals. So, in theory, there should be a steady reduction in the demand for laboratory animals. No way. There is no sign in a slackening of the demand for, say, specially bred white mice. In fact, the people who breed these things say that not only do they need to supply more, but they are having to provide specialist varieties for new and exotic uses, such as genetic engineering and testing ground breaking surgical techniques.

Public hypocrisy

We could continue to bemoan the fate of laboratory animals, while blithely accepting the benefits of their sacrifice. Or we could say that we won't use the products of companies that carry out animal tests at all. The third so-called option, promoted by outfits dedicated to finding alternatives, is in reality an acceptance that animal testing is necessary for the time being. So what should we do?

We should note, firstly, where the pressure for all this testing is coming from. From you and me, that's who. Most of us want to be reassured about the safety of the soap that our children use. If we aren't we won't buy it. On the other hand, not enough of us will pay the extra margin that would make other ways of testing economic.

Scientists who are working in medical research are at the centre of the controversy. Ironically, it is the men and women who turn down lucrative approaches from drugs companies on the grounds that they do not want their research compromised who often become the objects of attack by the wilder fringes of the animal welfare movement. Their argument is that if they could find easier, quicker ways of saving human beings from the effects of disease, ageing or contagion, they would do so. But which of us, told that our son or daughter has been diagnosed with cancer, would say "save the bunny rabbit, [damn] the child"?

World Lab Animal Day should be an opportunity for us to insist that animals are treated as humanely as possible, that we try hard to find alternatives to their use in experiments and that we do as little testing as is necessary. But let this be one more nail in the coffin of public hypocrisy. We love animals; but we love ourselves more, and we should admit it.

8

Animal Experimentation Should Be Guided by Humane Principles

Joanne Zurlo, Alan M. Goldberg, and Deborah Rudacille

Joanne Zurlo, Alan M. Goldberg, and Deborah Rudacille are associate director, director, and research writer, respectively, at the Center for Alternatives to Animal Testing, Johns Hopkins School of Public Health.

In the controversy surrounding animal experimentation, researchers must gain public confidence by showing that they treat lab animals well. This humane treatment should include a concern for limiting any pain or duress that these animals may suffer, and a desire to eliminate animal testing when alternative methods are available. Researchers are responsible for proving that their actions are guided by a compassionate regard for the animals in their care.

Independent surveys carried out over the past 15 years in the United States and Europe have consistently revealed that animal protection is no longer a fringe issue. However, relatively few in the widely defined animal-protection community identify themselves as "antivivisectionists."

In fact, a majority of U.S. and European citizens support animal research—when they see evidence that researchers respect laboratory animals, take animal pain and distress into consideration, and alleviate both whenever possible. Clearly, the logical way to build public support for research is for scientists to illustrate by word and deed that they value the animals in their care, and recognize both the moral and the scientific rationale for humane care and treatment of laboratory animals.

Attacks on animal protectionists do little to further the perception that researchers are responsible guardians of animal welfare. Instead, they reinforce a negative stereotype of scientists as individuals concerned solely with scientific challenges and unwilling to engage in serious ethical reflection and dialogue.

Such stereotypes serve to alienate legislators and members of the pub-

Reprinted from Joanne Zurlo, Alan M. Goldberg, and Deborah Rudacille, "Public Support for Research Depends on Humane Treatment of Lab Animals," *The Scientist*, vol. 10, no. 15, July 22, 1996, with permission.

lic, who consequently feel that scientists do not understand their concerns and are therefore incapable of safeguarding animal well-being without stringent oversight and regulation. Those scientists who dismiss animal protection virtually ensure that research will become more expensive, more unpopular, and more difficult.

The three Rs

There is, however, a middle ground, in which the need for animal research is acknowledged together with the recognition that animal welfare is a scientific, as well as a societal, consideration. Called the Three Rs, this approach emphasizes reduction, refinement, and replacement of animal use whenever possible. It was initially described by two British scientists, William M.S. Russell and Rex Burch, in their 1959 book, *The Principles of Humane Experimental Technique* (London, Methuen, 1959; reprinted in 1992 by the Universities Federation for Animal Welfare, Potters Bar, Herts, U.K.). In this book, they point out that "if we are to use a criterion for choosing experiments to perform, the criterion of humanity is the best we could possibly invent."

By "humanity," Russell and Burch meant optimum care of the animal. Laws requiring reduction, refinement, and replacement alternatives to animal use in science have been passed in the U.S. and Europe over the past decade. These laws place responsibility for the animals' well-being squarely in the hands of scientists and laboratory staff. A deeper understanding and more informed implementation of these principles is therefore not just ethically and scientifically correct, but also legislatively required (M. Balls, A.M. Goldberg, J.H. Fentem et al., *Alternatives to Laboratory Animals*, 23:838-66, 1995).

It is far easier to adopt one-dimensional slogans that reflect an all-or-nothing mentality than to address the complexity of the Three Rs approach. For that very reason, the principles of humane experimental technique pose an intellectual challenge, which scientists should embrace. The Three Rs offer an opportunity to enhance the scientific, economic, and ethical value of every experimental protocol.

Clearly, the logical way to build public support for research is for scientists to illustrate by word and deed that they value the animals in their care, and recognize both the moral and the scientific rationale for humane care and treatment of laboratory animals.

It is not enough that investigators know their treatment of laboratory animals is exemplary. They must be forthcoming in demonstrating to the public that they indeed care for these animals. They can do so by contributing articles and letters about laboratory experiences to the popular press. They can visit classrooms and talk to students not only about how animal research has benefited humankind, but also about how animal care and use are guided by the Three Rs. More scientists can attend meetings and participate in dialogues with the animal-protection community to focus not on the differences between the two groups, but on opportunities for collaborative efforts and shared concerns.

These efforts will help to demonstrate that scientists do care for their animal subjects humanely, because it is scientifically expedient to do so, and because they possess high standards of ethics. These actions can reinforce the image of a caring researcher who still needs to use animals to advance biomedical research, but who uses the fewest number of animals necessary, treats them with the utmost care to ensure they are free of pain, and replaces them with non-animal methods wherever possible. As Dartmouth scientist Bill D. Roebuck noted in a recent article in the *Johns Hopkins Center for Alternatives to Animal Testing Newsletter* (13[2]: 9, 1996), "one must always weigh tried and true procedures with newer ways of generating similar data. In comparison shopping between methods and experimental approaches, some new and better approaches may arise. More often, refinements of existing approaches will develop. The key point is that opportunities to enhance the scientific value of the experiment can be found in such a review process, while meeting the institutional and societal obligation."

Acknowledgment of the principles of the Three Rs is not an apology for using animals, but a reassurance that as long as it remains necessary to do so, nonhuman research subjects will be treated humanely and respectfully. The public perception of science will be greatly enhanced if our colleagues accept the challenge brought on by the Three Rs and the benefits that accompany it.

9

Animal Experimentation Needs Moral Justification

R.G. Frey

R.G. Frey is a professor of philosophy at Bowling Green University in Ohio.

Because animal lives have value, ethical persons should question whether animal experimentation is justified. The comparative quality of life between animals and humans may help explain why humans feel less troubled about inflicting pain on animals. However, such assessments invite a logical argument that would sanction experimenting on some humans who have a lower quality of life than their peers. Finding the moral ground for justifying animal experimentation is not easy and is therefore often overlooked. Scientists and society as a whole need to confront this dilemma.

From teaching to research, the use we make of animals in human health care is vast. Although it is always possible that the animals themselves may benefit from this use (in fact, they rarely do), the search for health-care benefits for ourselves motivates it. This raises an ethical problem: What justifies this systematic use of animals for human gain? Most of us who think some or much animal experimentation in medicine justified do not address this question, and this strikes me as a mistake on three counts.

First, the question demands an answer, if we are morally serious people. We owe a justification for how it is we engage in, support, and make use of the results of experimental practices that we openly concede involve the deliberate, intentional infliction of pain and suffering and/or death on other feeling creatures. Second, failure to address the question leaves the field clear for antivivisectionists to dominate it, not only in the media but also in the general area of argumentation for and against the practices in question. Third, failure to address the question implicitly leaves a suspicion in people's minds that justification of our use of animals in human health care cannot be given, that, as it were, we simply use our power and dominion over animals for our own ends without any justification.

Justifying what humans do to animals

I have attempted, in a series of publications, to sketch a justification for much (but not all) of what we do to animals in the name of human health care.[1] This task is not an easy one, however, and anyone who offers up a simple nostrum that shows how right we are to lay waste to the other creatures of the earth has not fully grasped the nature of the task. In what follows, I want to show how one important complication arises, if we continue to justify animal experimentation in the way we usually do.[2]

First, however, a word on why some obvious ploys to avoid our question carry little conviction. Animals use each other, so why should we not use them? Because we are reflective creatures capable of moral thought and moral assessment of our actions; nothing follows about the rightness of killing creatures who are not thus capable (babies, the severely mentally subnormal, animals). If your child were dying, would you not want any and all animal experimentation done, if the child could be saved? Yes, I would, but that is precisely why we do not do our reflective moral thinking in the heat of the moment, when we might want every penny in the land spent on our child.

Does not the law permit us, given approved protocols and project licenses, to experiment on animals? Yes, it does, but it also permits us to stand on shore and watch a man drown. In certain cases, we expect more of ourselves than merely what the law permits; morality can apply even when the law does not. This is particularly true when what we do is deliberately, intentionally done. We are morally responsible for what we deliberately, intentionally do, whatever the state of the law, and everyone involved in and supportive of medical research knows this.

A last ploy leads us to the heart of the matter. This ploy consists in the claim that animals do not count morally. This claim looks odd, however, in the light of the way medical researchers themselves behave today. For it is their standard practice, as ethics review committees, journal and peer review procedures, and the like all insist, to seek to ensure that animal pain and suffering are controlled, that they are limited so far as possible, that they are mitigated with drugs where feasible, and that they be justified in the course and by the nature of the experiment proposed. Oversight committees, including governmental ones, can now shut down research where these matters are ignored.

If animal life has even some value, then its deliberate destruction or the drastic lowering of its quality is something morally serious people must address.

If, however, one thinks animal suffering counts, then it seems very odd to think that animal lives do not; the worry about pain and suffering in part is simply the worry about the very negative drawbacks to a life that they impose, whether in humans or animals. Unless we thought that those lives had some value, it is hard to see why we would care about ruining them or severely lowering their quality or why we would go to such great lengths to cite the actual or potential benefits that justify their sacrifice. But if animal life has even some value, then its deliberate destruction or the drastic lowering of its quality is something morally serious people must address.

But surely, someone will insist, our morality cannot prevent us from preserving our own lives. No, of course, it cannot; the issue is how far we can go in preserving our lives. What are the limits? We ask this question even in the human case, when we ponder what, in order to save our own lives or enhance the quality of our lives, we may do to others. So one cannot look the question of limits away.

Having come this far, we can see why what animal liberationists call "speciesism" cannot be part of these limits. In the play *Equus*, a man goes around blinding horses; it seems extraordinary to claim that his doing this to children is wrong, whereas his doing it to horses is not. Pain is pain, whatever the creature that experiences it. Nor do I expect many people today at bottom think differently: Even if it were true, legally, that a horse could be whipped to death with impunity at one time in our country, I doubt that such an act was ever thought morally above reproach.

Pain is pain, whatever the creature that experiences it.

The situation, then, seems to me to be this: Where pain and suffering are concerned, I can see no difference between the human and animal cases; where the destruction of valuable lives is concerned, those who destroy these valuable things owe us an explanation of how it can possibly be that species membership suffices to distinguish morally between two relevantly similar acts of killing. Although not an animal liberationist, then, I can see their point here.

Suppose we focus on killing: The boundaries to our discussion are clear. Animals count, morally; their lives have some value; and the destruction of these valuable things requires justification. This concern with the value of animal lives in turn raises the question of the comparative value of human and animal life, and one of the great virtues of my position on this issue is that it coheres nicely with recent discussions of the value of life in medical ethics and allied areas. That is, what matters is not life but quality of life. The value of a life is a function of its quality, its quality of its richness, and its richness of its capacities and scope for enrichment; it matters, then, what a creature's capacities for a rich life are.

Here, the human and animal cases differ. The question is not, say, whether a chicken's life has value; I agree that it does. The chicken has an unfolding series of experiences and can suffer, and it is perfectly capable of living out a life appropriate to its species. The question is whether the chicken's life approaches normal adult human life in quality (and so value), given its capacities and the life that is appropriate to its species, and this is a matter of the comparative value of such lives. It is in this context that the claim that normal adult human life is more valuable than animal life occurs, and I defend it on the ground of the greater richness and potentialities for enrichment in the human case.

One must be careful here not to resort to a kind of extreme skepticism, namely, that we can know nothing of the richness of animal lives.

A good deal of recent work by ethologists and animal behaviorists, including those very sympathetic to the "animal rights" case, such as Marian Dawkins[3] and Donald Griffin,[4] would seem to show that we can know something of the richness and quality of life of "higher" animals. That we cannot know everything in no way implies that we cannot know a good deal.

Quality-of-life views

Quality-of-life views of the sort described[5] turn upon richness, and if we are to answer the question of the comparative value of human and animal life we must inquire after the richness of their respective lives. Intraspecies comparisons are sometimes difficult, as we learn in medical ethics, when we try to judge the respective quality of life of each of two human lives; but such comparisons are not completely beyond us. They are made every day in our hospitals in allocating resources. Interspecies comparisons of richness and quality of life are likely to be even more difficult, though again not impossible.

I agree that, as we descend from the "higher" animals, we are likely to lose all behavioral correlates that we use to gain access to the interior lives of animals. Yet, scientific work increasingly appears that gives us a glimpse into animal lives, though it is hard as yet to make out much of a claim of extensive richness on the strength of this work. On this count, ethologists are usually cautious.

In trying to judge the richness and quality of an animal's life, we must exercise care in two further directions. First, we must not use in some unreflective manner criteria appropriate for assessing the richness of human lives as if they applied straightforwardly to the animal case. Rather, we must use all that we know about animals, especially those closest to us, to try to gauge the quality of their lives in terms appropriate to their species. Then, we must try to gauge the differences we allude to when we say, first of a chicken, then of a fellow human, that each has led a rich, full life. The fullest chicken life there has ever been, so science suggests, does not approach the full life of a human; the differences in capacities are just too great.

[A] man's life is more valuable than [a] chicken's because of its higher quality, greater enrichment, and greater scope for enrichment.

Second, if one nevertheless wants to maintain, as some animal liberationists would seem to want to do, that the chicken's life is equally as valuable as the life of a normal adult human, then it must be true that, whatever the capacities of the chicken and however limited those capacities may be, they confer a richness upon the chicken's life that approximates the richness of the human's life, despite all the different and additional capacities present in the typical human case. Evidence is needed to support this claim, because by its behavior alone we will not ordinarily think this of a chicken.

Of course, we share many activities with chickens; we eat, sleep, and reproduce. But such activities do not exhaust the richness of lives with music, art, literature, culture generally, love, science, and all the many products and joys of reflection. Indeed, even this list does not take account of how we fashion our lives into and so live out lives of striving to exemplify excellences of various sorts, whether as painters, ball players, or plumbers. These are ways of living that are themselves sources of value to us. No chicken has ever lived thus.

One might try to retain a quality-of-life view of the value of a life but drop the provision that quality be determined by richness; in this way, one might seek to block my judgment of reduced richness in the animal case. But if quality of life is not to be determined by richness—that is, by the extent, variety, and quality of experiences—I do not know what else is to determine it. Certainly, there is nothing else cited in those quality-of-life views with which I am familiar.

We cannot pretend that the only way human health care gains can be achieved is through experimenting on animals; we could, of course, experiment on humans.

Why not opt, it might be asked, for a much simpler view: The chicken and the man have different capacities and lives; judged by their respective capacities, each leads a full, though different, life. The problem here has a deeper aspect: One seems to be saying that these lives, and so the ingredients that make up these lives, are in some sense incommensurable, when, in fact, the central ingredients, experiences and the unfolding of experiences in a life, appear remarkably alike.

Can I know what it's like to be a dog? More or less. And this is why I believe playing fetch with it enriches its life. Can I know exactly the degree to which fetch enriches its life? No, just as I sometimes cannot know the degree of enrichment in the case of humans. But I have absolutely no reason to believe that the dog's life possesses anything like the variety and depth of ways of enrichment that my life possesses, and I especially need evidence to make me believe that the enrichment of the dog's life through any one of its capacities can make up for this extensive variety and depth in my case. The eagle can see farther and deeper than I can, but how does this fact transform the richness of its life to approximate the richness that the variety and depth of my capacities confer upon me? I need evidence to believe that it does.

Killing and the value of life

Why all this matters should be obvious: If killing is related to the value of a life, then I can explain why we think that killing a man is worse than killing a chicken and in a way that does not rely upon species membership to account for the wrongness of killing. Whatever the full account of this matter, a part of it seems clearly bound up with our view that the man's life is more valuable than the chicken's life. And I can explain this issue of value also in a nonspeciesist way: The man's life is more valuable than the chicken's because of its higher quality, greater enrichment, and greater scope for enrichment.

This explanation allows that the chicken's life has some value; what it denies is that the chicken's life has the same value as the man's. Here, then, is how we might approach the killing of animals, and it is an account that coheres nicely with quality-of-life views that we encounter regularly in many areas and aspects of medical ethics and life.

Obviously, all the above needs to be filled out in much greater detail, including factual, scientific detail; but it should be clear that something along the lines of this sketch is widely endorsed by many of us in dealing with the value of lives. For example, we think about the quality of our lives and often say today that, even if we could be kept alive in some reduced state or other, we would not wish to be so sustained if the quality of our lives slipped disastrously. This leads to the complication in the argument I noted at the outset.

The quality of human life

Not all human life is of the same quality and richness. We all know this either firsthand or through the media, as cases appear in which the quality of a life has slipped so disastrously that questions are raised about whether that life is worth preserving. And these questions are being raised increasingly by the very people living those lives, as cases of requested physician-assisted death illustrate.

All of us know that some human lives are so tragic that we would not wish them on our worst enemy, and it seems mere pretense to go on about how valuable such a life is. In the abstract, each human life is often held to be precious, but anyone who has ever been around a hospital knows that some human lives are of such a low quality as to be massively below the quality of normal adult life. We can thus explain why it is worse to kill a man than a chicken when the quality of the human life in question approaches that of normal adult human life, but we must face the fact that not all human lives are of the quality and value of normal adult human life.

The fact that not all human life is equally valuable is a serious one. For we cannot pretend that the only way human health care gains can be achieved is through experimenting on animals; we could, of course, experiment on humans. That is, we must face the fact that the quality of a human life can fall so far below the quality of normal adult human life as even to fall below the quality of life of a perfectly healthy animal.

What, then, justifies our using the animal in preference to the human in experiments, given that the benefit from the experiment can be had by experimenting on either one? (Indeed, to the extent that animal models are less reliable than human models for humans, one might think there were even additional gains to be had from using the human.) What we need is obvious: We need to be able to appeal to something that ensures that a human life of any quality, however low, exceeds in value an animal life of any quality, however high, in circumstances in which the human life has plummeted to a tragic degree. Unfortunately, I know of no such thing.

Now let me hasten to add that I am not advocating experiments on these unfortunate humans who are among the weakest among us. What I am trying to show is that, by the logic of our argument, we are forced to envisage such experiments, if, and I stress this, we continue to appeal to the benefits of experimentation and we rely upon the comparative value of human and animal life to show why these benefits cannot be realized through experimenting on humans. So far as I can see, if we continue with animal experiments on this basis, our argument forces us to consider experiments on humans, unless, and again I repeat the point, one knows of something that ensures that a human life of any quality, however tragically low, is more valuable than an animal life of any quality, however very high. I know of nothing of this kind.

To be sure, one might say here that I could obtain what I seek if only I believed in God and accepted a religion. Then, I could tell a story in which, however convenient it may otherwise appear, God has made it true that human lives are always, and in every condition, more valuable than animal lives. I do not doubt that one may find comfort in this thought, but what if one does not? Besides, it seems to require medical researchers to believe in God and God's handiwork on our behalf, in order to explain why they use animals of a high quality of life in preference to humans of a very low quality of life, and medical researchers are by no means all religious believers.

Finally, we come to a simple thought: Why can we just not say that we prefer our own kind to another and give that as our reason for not using humans? I do not have space to go into this thought adequately, but two obvious points leap out at once. First, how are we to define our own kind? If I say human, as opposed to animal or rodent, one may agree, but what if I say white male as opposed to black male? Presumably, one does not agree. So how do we tell which references to our own kind are acceptable morally and which are not? The answer is not obvious.

Although I am not an antivivisectionist or animal liberationist . . ., I am troubled by this matter of providing a justification of what we deliberately, intentionally do to animals.

Second, we start out trying to use quality-of-life arguments to show why it is worse to kill humans than animals and then, once we realize that we might face hard cases, turn around, cite a preference for our own kind, and dispense with quality-of-life arguments in our justification of killing animals in the name of human health care. So what justification is left us? Some answer must be given, particularly in light of the vast discrepancies in quality of life between some healthy animals and some massively unfortunate humans; otherwise, we will not have given a justification of animal experimentation at all.

Accordingly, although I am not an antivivisectionist or animal liberationist and though I certainly want the medical benefits that flow from animal experimentation to continue, I am troubled by this matter of providing a justification of what we deliberately, intentionally do to animals.

If one does not like the justification (really, the barest outline of one) attempted here, or if another is not forthcoming, or if another contains mere assertion of the greater value of our lives or mere dogma about our superiority, then how can we continue with what we are doing?

Footnotes:

1. "Vivisection, Medicine, and Morals," *Journal of Medical Ethics* 9 (1983); "Animal Parts, Human Wholes: On the Use of Animals as a Source of Organs for Human Transplant," in J.M. Humber, R.F. Almeder, eds., *Biomedical Ethics Reviews* (Clifton, N.J.: Humana Press, 1987); "The Significance of Agency and Marginal Cases," *Philosophica* 39 (1987); "Autonomy and the Value of Animal Life," *The Monist* 70 (1987); "Moral Standing, The Value of Lives, and Speciesism," *Between the Species* 4 (1988); "Animals, Science, and Morality," *Behavioral and Brain Sciences* 13 (1990); "The Ethics of the Search for Benefits: Animal Experimentation in Medicine," in R. Gillon, ed., *Principles of Health Care Ethics* (New York: John Wiley, 1993). For background reading on the ethical theory out of which my views come, see my *Interests and Rights* (Oxford: Clarendon Press, 1980) and *Rights, Killing, and Suffering* (Oxford: Basil Blackwell, 1983).

2. It will become apparent below what I mean by "the way we do"; namely, by appeal to the benefits that animal experimentation brings and by reliance upon claims about the comparative value of human and animal life to avoid experimenting on humans.

3. See her *Animal Suffering* (London: Chapman and Hall, 1980) and *Through Our Eyes Only: The Search for Animal Consciousness* (Oxford: W.H. Freeman, 1993).

4. See his *Animal Minds* (Chicago: University of Chicago Press, 1992).

5. Different accounts of quality of life are possible, including, as I note in the text, one that treats the notion of richness differently.

10

Animal Experimentation Is Unscientific

Javier B. Burgos

Javier B. Burgos is the president of The Nature of Wellness, an organization devoted to informing the public about the medical and scientific invalidity of animal experimentation and testing.

Since every species is unique, it is absurd to believe that human diseases or ailments can be cured by applying information garnered from animal experimentation. Animal models have not supplied useful information about threatening human diseases such as AIDS, cross-species transplants have ended in costly failures, and drugs tested safe on animals have proven deadly when consumed by humans. Common sense should dictate that these medical tactics are unsound and potentially disastrous.

If your dog Fido got sick and were dying, do you think it would be scientifically possible, and I mean scientifically possible, to find a cure for your dog by conducting research on your healthy uncle Walter?

This extremely simple question illustrates the total absurdity on which today's biomedical research is based. Clearly, since it is not possible to cure a sick animal by conducting research on healthy human beings, curing sick human beings by experimenting on healthy animals is equally impossible.

The reasons behind this argument are overwhelmingly simple. First, every species of animal is a totally different biomechanical and biochemical entity. Therefore, it is impossible to extrapolate data not only from non-human animals to human beings, but also, from one species of animal to another. Second, it is impossible to recreate a spontaneous disease in the laboratory, whether it be on humans or on animals. Clearly, "recreated" and "spontaneous" are contradictory terms. The only exception to this is the case of infectious diseases. However, animals do not get human infectious diseases and we do not get theirs. This explains why animal experimenters have not been able to give AIDS to a single non-human animal.

Tragically for us all, the biomedical establishment operates in total defiance of these two most fundamental principles. Its research is based on the theory of "the animal model of human disease" which maintains that it is possible to reproduce spontaneous human diseases such as cardiovascular diseases, diabetes, cancer, muscular dystrophy, Alzheimer's disease, AIDS, etc., on healthy, non-human animals.

The pseudo-scientific belief that human medicine can be based on veterinary medicine has led the biomedical establishment to engage in other absurdities, such as the transplantation of bone marrow from baboons into human beings, xenotransplantation or interspecies organ transplantation (attempted since 1905 with predictably catastrophic results), artificial organ transplantation which has also ended in total and costly failure, and genetic manipulation which—like all fantasies—is based on wishful thinking rather than on cold scientific facts.

The arguments against animal experimentation

The medical and scientific arguments against animal experimentation are irrefutable. But no one should have to take our word for it. The evidence is all around us:

After decades of massive animal-based research at a cost of billions of tax dollars, crippling and deadly diseases of all kinds are affecting an ever-increasing number of Americans. In the U.S., the annual price tag for what is euphemistically called "health care" has already surpassed the one trillion dollar mark ($1,000,000,000,000)—14% of the American economy. It is conservatively estimated that, beginning in the year 2000, the annual U.S. health care bill will reach the $2 trillion mark, and an incredible $16 trillion a year by the time the year 2030 rolls around—a staggering 32% of the projected U.S. economy.

The obvious question is this: If animal research works, then why is it that the "miracle cures" and the "medical breakthroughs" that are always "around the corner" never materialize?

> *Clearly, since it is not possible to cure a sick animal by conducting research on healthy human beings, curing sick human beings by experimenting on healthy animals is equally impossible.*

In fact, we are going backwards! Take cancer, for example. Since President Nixon launched the "war on cancer" back in 1971, and after spending countless billions of tax dollars infecting millions of perfectly healthy animals with artificially-induced cancerous tumors, the rate of cancer incidence has gone up by 18% and cancer deaths have increased by 7%. Birth defects have skyrocketed in the last 40 years. Presently, 1 child in 7 is born with some kind of birth defect. The U.S. ranks at the unhealthy bottom of every health statistic, whether it be in connection with infant mortality or longevity. We rank number 1 in one category, however. We spend more money per capita on "health care" than any other nation in the world.

Pharmaceutical drugs found "safe" for human consumption based on animal tests often cause massive damage and even death. If animal testing is a valid way of assessing human reactions to drugs, then why do so many serious side effects remain unknown until the human "guinea pig" is exposed to the drug?

The fact is that animals react differently to different substances, not only from human beings, but also from each other. Aspirin kills cats and penicillin kills guinea pigs. Yet, the same guinea pigs can safely eat strychnine—one of the deadliest poisons for humans, but not for monkeys. Sheep can swallow enormous quantities of arsenic—once the murderers' favorite poison. Potassium cyanide, deadly for humans, is harmless for the owl. The list is endless.

Increasing numbers of doctors and scientists agree that the methodology of today's biomedical research is invalid and counterproductive.

The massive production and widespread use of pesticides (there are 40,000 different types currently being used in the U.S.) and countless other chemicals—deemed "safe" by U.S. regulatory agencies following massive animal tests—cause the pollution of our land, air, rivers, and oceans. The consequent poisoning of our food and water supplies, the destruction of the earth's protective ozone layer and many other threats are jeopardizing the very survival of life on our planet.

The logical course of medical research

Increasing numbers of doctors and scientists agree that the methodology of today's biomedical research is invalid and counterproductive. They further agree that there are only two ways to deal with human health problems: First, and foremost, we must learn how to practice prevention. The fact remains that an overwhelming number of diseases can be prevented by the adoption of appropriate diets, healthy lifestyles, and the elimination of environmental toxins. This is by far the most intelligent choice and deserves the lion's share of our resources.

Once people get sick, the only way to gather reliable and thus useful information is to examine the patients who have the actual disease. Only this vital information, obtainable through human clinical research (and not through experimental research on animals), can lead to effective treatments and real cures.

Many prominent doctors, scientists, politicians, and community and business leaders who understand the madness of basing human medicine on veterinary medicine, have never spoken out publicly in favor of phasing out animal experimentation. I am pleading with them to do so now. But, above all, I am pleading with the millions of Americans who already know that something is terribly wrong with animal experimentation. It is time for us all to demand a medicine based on logic and common sense. It is not only the right thing to do. It is the only thing that can save us from an impending disaster, euphemistically called "health care crisis."

11

Animal Experimentation Has Hindered AIDS Research

Peter Tatchell

Peter Tatchell is a leading activist with the Gay Liberation Front, an organization formed to expose and fight discrimination against homosexuals. He is also one of the founders of Outrage!, a London-based organization of homosexual activists. He has published several books and articles.

In the 1990s, the testing of AIDS drugs on animals yielded false results that needlessly held up the distribution of life-saving protease inhibitors. To rely on animal testing as a means of approving the safety of AIDS drugs is ridiculous because animals and humans have different physiologies. AIDS is a uniquely human disease; money that is spent on animal research in the name of fighting the disease is being filtered away from research that may actually find a cure.

The development of life-saving protease inhibitors was delayed for four years by the pharmaceutical company Merck because the drugs killed laboratory dogs and rats, according to the *Washington Post Magazine*, (1-May-1997). During those four years, tens of thousands of people with AIDS who would have benefited from protease inhibitors died needlessly. Many would now be alive if Merck had not engaged in animal research and made the false assumption that data gathered from other species can be applied to humans. This scandal is further evidence that animal experimentation is hindering the fight against AIDS.

People and animals have vastly different physiologies. Scientific results gathered from animal studies cannot therefore be generalised to humans, as the following two examples illustrate.

- Strychnine is harmless to monkeys, but lethal to humans.
- Penicillin kills guinea pigs, but not people.

HIV is a uniquely human disease: it doesn't affect any other species the way it affects humans. The surest way of discovering a vaccine and a cure is by researching the interaction of HIV with the human immune

Reprinted from Peter Tatchell, "Animal Research Delayed Protease Inhibitors for Four Years," *Outrage!* (1997), www.outrage.cygnet.co.uk/protease.htm, with permission.

system, not the immune systems of animals.

This recognition is now prompting some AIDS activists to argue that experiments with other species are holding back the development of safer, more-effective anti-HIV drugs. One of Britain's top researchers, Prof. Robin Weiss, has expressed serious doubt that information gathered from studies of laboratory animals can help illuminate the mechanisms by which HIV sabotages the immunity of humans. Another senior AIDS doctor in Britain has described the millions of dollars spent on animal research as "almost criminally negligent" because it is diverting resources away from more promising avenues of molecular-level research with human cells and the HIV virus.

A similar view has been expressed by Dr. Albert Sabin, the inventor of the first oral polio vaccine. He was quoted in London's *Independent on Sunday* newspaper as saying, "what has been demonstrated up to now in animals does not have any relevance."

The surest way of discovering a vaccine and a cure [for AIDS] is by researching the interaction of HIV with the human immune system, not the immune systems of animals.

In the United States, Prof. Patricia Fultz, who was a senior scientist in the Centers for Disease Control and Prevention's chimpanzee AIDS research programme, admits she now has doubts that experimentation with other species can help us understand or treat HIV in humans, (as reported in *Science* magazine, 13-October-1995).

The director of AIDS research at Duke University, Dani Bolognesi, has had second thoughts too. Writing in the June 1994 *Journal of NIH Research*, Bolognesi argued that animal studies do not provide a reliable indicator of how HIV affects people and how the disease can be conquered. "No animal models faithfully reproduce human immune deficiency virus-type (HIV-1) infection and disease in humans," wrote Bolognesi. "Animals are not optimal models."

Animal research has not helped

The fact is that all the current and forthcoming anti-HIV treatments were developed as a result of human-based cellular research, which showed us how HIV locks onto and penetrates human cells, and the mechanism by which HIV produces new infectious virus particles within these human cells. None of these breakthroughs was achieved by research with other species.

Indeed, a significant human-based breakthrough in AIDS research, made in Britain in 1989, was partly funded by the animal rights charity The Dr. Hadwen Trust for Humane Research. This discovery of how HIV enters human cells might not have been achieved, according to the research team headed by Prof. Jonathan Weber at St. Mary's Hospital in London, if they had concentrated on experiments with chimpanzees and other animals, as did many of their medical colleagues.

So far as drug toxicity is concerned, the unreliability of safety-testing HIV drugs on other species has been confirmed by a seven-year study involving 84 laboratories worldwide, coordinated by the University of Uppsala in Sweden. Known as the Multicenter Evaluation of In vitro Cytotoxicology (MEIC) study, it shows that human cells are 22% more accurate in predicting toxicity than whole live laboratory animals. This makes testing new anti-HIV drugs on animals redundant. Human cell tests give faster, more-precise results.

Moreover, because humans and animals react differently to drug therapies, there is the risk that animal testing might result in dangerous or ineffective anti-HIV drugs being approved and in less than fully efficacious doses being prescribed. Let us never forget the scandals of Opren, Thalidomide, and AZT, which were declared "safe" after extensive animal research.

12

Animals Are Poor Models in Cancer Research

Animal Alliance of Canada

The Animal Alliance of Canada is an animal rights advocacy and education group which focuses on local, regional, national and international issues concerning the goodwill and respectful treatment of animals by humans.

Animal models have failed to provide useful information concerning the contracting and spread of cancer in humans. In fact, a reliance on animal models may blind some researchers to the significant differences between the way in which cancer develops and travels in humans and animals. Regardless, cancer is best fought through prevention rather than after-the-fact treatments. Money spent on animal-related cancer research could better be spent on prevention programs that stress diet and lifestyle changes.

R esearch to find a cure for cancer is a lucrative business. North American budget for the "war against cancer" exceeded $1 billion annually in the mid-1990s and continues to grow. A significant portion of this sum is devoted to animal experimentation. However, increasing numbers of scientists and lay-people now recognize that studying human cancers on animals is pointless and misleading. Furthermore, after-the-fact treatment is much less effective and cost-efficient than prevention programs stressing diet and lifestyle.

Animal models

Studying human cancer on animals is cruel and useless. For example, despite evidence in the 1800's that coal tar causes human skin cancer, researchers denied this correlation for 150 years because they couldn't induce cancer in animals painted with coal tar. Similarly, animal experimenters wasted 50 years looking for a cure for breast cancer before bio-statisticians looking at human data realized that women do not die from breast cancer itself, but as a result of the cancer spreading. Animal

Reprinted from "Animal Experimentation and Cancer Research," an electronic article on the website of Animal Alliance of Canada: www.animalalliance.ca/cancer.htm, with permission.

models did not reveal this crucial information because cancer artificially induced in laboratory animals does not naturally spread.

The Medical Research Modernization Committee (MRMC) reviewed 10 animal models, chosen randomly by computer, in order to determine the general value of animal models for human medicine. The study concluded that none of the models appeared to provide "significant contributions to the diagnosis, prevention, understanding or treatment of the human diseases for which they were studied. Upon reviewing the data we concluded that using an animal model . . . is a logically flawed process." This study went on to point out that researchers who use animal models often ignore anatomical, physiological and pathological differences between humans and other animals because they focus on specific similarities of the disease process in humans and animals. This method provides misleading results. Disease affects almost all functioning and interacting elements of an animal. Thus, "focusing on one aspect of a disease fails to account for the actual complexity of biological systems."

Increasing numbers of scientists and lay-people now recognize that studying human cancers on animals is pointless and misleading.

Ophthalmologist Dr. Stephen Kaufman of the MRMC criticizes animal models on the grounds that they do not approximate human diseases. Kaufman states that the "injection of rapidly dividing cancers into young, healthy rodents creates cancers very different from the spontaneous, slow-growing tumors that are the major cause of terminal cancers in elderly humans." Furthermore, inducing cancer in otherwise healthy animals does not help researchers to address the important point that human cancer reflects a failure of the immune system.

Dr. Irwin Bross, a respected cancer specialist, states emphatically that "from a scientific standpoint, what are called animal model systems in cancer research have been a total failure . . . because there is no animal model system which resembles the human cancer process." Dr. Bross also stresses that animal models have not resulted in the development of a single drug to treat cancer. All widely used cancer treatment drugs were first detected through clinical use and then were tested on animals. Similarly, most human carcinogens were revealed through epidemiological studies, not through animal experiments.

Dr. John Bailar of McGill University's medical faculty agrees with Dr. Bross. Dr. Bailar's report for the federal Laboratory Centre for Disease Control, published in *Chronic Diseases in Canada*, states that "the long history of [cancer] research that has focused almost exclusively on treatment has not produced the benefits that we all hoped and expected to see." This report stresses the necessity for a whole new approach to cancer which emphasizes preventing the disease through lifestyle changes and diet.

Dr. Bross sums up the research situation by pointing out that the myth that animal models have resulted in effective cancer treatments perpetuates the cancer industry's multi-billion dollar funding. Thus, "even though the historical facts show that animal experiments were worse than useless in selecting clinically effective cancer chemotherapies the 'consensus of authorities' will continue to say just the opposite."

Diet and cancer prevention

For 30 years, the American Cancer Society told people to "Fight cancer with a check-up and a cheque." This slogan represents the nonexistence of prevention in traditional cancer treatment. This policy is inexcusable considering that studies have consistently indicated that 80% of all cancers are related to lifestyle and environmental factors and are therefore preventable. These factors include smoking, drinking alcohol, eating meat, fatty foods and food additives, and exposure to pollutants and industrial chemicals. Studies suggest that tobacco causes approximately 30% of cancers, diet 40–60%.

High cancer rates are intrinsically linked with fat consumption, particularly of animal fats. North Americans consume more fat than most other people in the world. As our consumption of meat, poultry, dairy products and vegetable oils have increased over the years, so too have our cancer rates.

Women in Japan, who traditionally eat very little meat, have the lowest rates of breast cancer in the world. In a landmark study, researchers tracked the cancer rates of Japanese immigrants to the U.S. and their children. Many Japanese women move to the U.S. and marry within their community, but adopt meat-based diets. This study showed that although the immigrant population remained relatively unchanged genetically, breast cancer rates nevertheless soared to equal those of neighbouring Caucasian women. According to Dr. Oliver Alabaster, Director of the Institute for Disease Prevention, "This is very dramatic evidence that cancer is mainly environmentally induced, rather than genetically inherited."

The precise role of fat in the development of cancer is unclear. One hypothesis suggests that fat influences the transportation of carcinogens into cells, another that fat may affect hormone levels and activity. What is clear, as a result of clinical studies, is that eating a high-fibre, vegetable-based diet, and significantly reducing our intake of animal-based products as well as saturated and unsaturated fats, reduces our risk of cancer. The bottom line, as expressed by the British Cancer Control Society, is that "Economics and politics simply intertwine in shaping conventional medicine's approach to cancer. Very simply put, treating disease is enormously profitable, preventing disease is not."

What you can do

1. Become a vegetarian, or better still, a vegan. This will not only reduce your risk of cancer and other diseases, but will also alleviate animal suffering and help the environment. Contact Animal Alliance or a vegetarian association in your area for more information about vegetarianism.

2. Do not donate money to charities that support animal research. See Animal Alliance's information sheet on charities which do not fund animal research.

3. Write letters to the editor explaining your position on animal research.

The importance of cancer prevention

Despite overwhelming evidence condemning the current strategies of the "war against cancer," billions of dollars are still being spent on inducing cancer in animals in the vain hope of finding a cure for this frightening disease. Study after study has shown that using animal models to study human cancer is inappropriate and even dangerous. Furthermore, since most cancers are related to lifestyle and environmental factors, focusing on preventing this disease would be a much more appropriate and effective strategy than using animal models to search for cures. Cancer researchers over the years have spent billions of dollars, harmed and killed millions of animals and misled countless people by refusing to acknowledge the importance of preventing cancer through a healthy lifestyle. As taxpayers and concerned citizens, it is up to each of us to insist that future cancer research focus on clinical studies and prevention education.

13

Animal-to-Human Transplants Are Ineffective

Alix Fano, Murry J. Cohen, Marjorie Cramer, Ray Greek, and Stephen R. Kaufman

Alix Fano, Murry J. Cohen, Marjorie Cramer, Ray Greek, and Stephen R. Kaufman are members of the Medical Research Modernization Committee (MRMC), a national health advocacy group composed of physicians, scientists, and other health care professionals who evaluate the benefits, risks, and costs of medical research methods and technologies.

Since the early twentieth century, scientists have been attempting to use animal organs to replace damaged or failed human organs. Such xenotransplantation (transplants that occur between different species) is expensive and the results are unpredictable and potentially deadly. The possibility of dangerous animal viruses being transferred to humans is great, and the track record for successful transplants is poor. Doctors should concentrate on proven alternatives, such as stressing preventative medicine, to improve human health.

The alleged chronic shortage of human organs has led some researchers and federal health officials in the US and elsewhere to consider using animals, such as pigs and nonhuman primates, as alternate sources of organs for humans. The prospect of commercial cross-species transplantation (or xenotransplantation)—attempted since the early 20th century—has created huge financial incentives for biotechnology and pharmaceutical companies. While some researchers and animal research advocates are optimistic about xenotransplantation's potential, others are calling for a moratorium on the technology, which they say threatens public health and the environment, has an appalling track record, and is both expensive and unnecessary. These concerns have not been satisfactorily addressed by xenotransplantation's proponents, who have overstated the technology's potential benefits.

Reprinted, with permission, from Alix Fano, Murry J. Cohen, Marjorie Cramer, Ray Greek, and Stephen R. Kaufman, "Of Pigs, Primates, and Plagues: A Layperson's Guide to the Problems with Animal-to-Human Organ Transplants," an electronic article on the website of the Medical Research Modernization Committee: www.mrmcmed.org/pigs.html.

Problems with xenotransplantation

Organ xenotransplantation's track record: 100% failure. There have been some 55 animal-to-human whole organ transplants attempted since 1906. All have proven unsuccessful, resulting in the suffering and death of all patients and donor animals. The thousands of cross-species experiments (between goats, rats and chickens, rats and hamsters, cats and dogs, pigs and primates) performed since 1906, and continuing today, have not provided reliable information about what would happen to human xenograft recipients. Xenotransplantation is a dangerous and unproven technology.

Xenotransplantation is expensive. Xenotransplantation is riskier and promises to be even more expensive than human-to-human transplantation ($250,000 per operation in 1995, not including the hidden costs of breeding, housing, feeding, medicating, testing, transporting, rendering, and disposing of the waste and remains of herds of transgenic animals). Institute of Medicine figures from 1996 reveal that xenotransplant costs for all patients who need organs could reach $20.3 billion. These costs are beyond the means of the majority of Americans and an already overburdened health care system. If ever successful, the technology would, at best, benefit a small minority of patients (100,000) while dramatically driving up health care costs for all.

The viral threat

We should learn from the past. Responsible public health authorities would steer clear of xenotransplantation in the interest of human health, particularly in light of the knowledge that animal viruses can jump the species barrier and kill humans. HIV—the virus that causes AIDS—may be a simian immunodeficiency virus (SIV) that leapt the species barrier in central Africa. Health authorities were unable to prevent the worldwide spread of HIV infection. Similarly, they were unable to prevent Ebola outbreaks in Sudan, Zaire (1976, 1979, 1995) and the US (1989, 1996). Furthermore, there is evidence that humans have become ill after consuming or being injected with animal materials. There is a reported link between the smallpox vaccine (derived from animal cells) and AIDS, a recently acknowledged link between human lung, brain and bone cancer and the SV (simian virus) 40 (found in old batches of the Salk polio vaccine), and the threat of emerging infectious diseases, including human Creutzfeldt-Jakob Disease (CJD) from the consumption of "mad cows" in Europe, the Netherlands, and the US.

> *There have been some 55 animal-to-human whole organ transplants attempted since 1906. All have proven unsuccessful, resulting in the suffering and death of all patients and donor animals.*

Why nonhuman primates should not be used as organ "donors." Baboon viruses flourish on human tissue cultures, before killing the cultures.

There are over 20 known, potentially lethal viruses that can be transmitted from nonhuman primates to humans, including Ebola, Marburg, hepatitis A and B, herpes B, SV40, and SIV. Numerous scientists have urged US public health agencies to exclude primates as donors for xenotransplantation.

Why pigs should not be used as organ "donors." Given the acknowledged danger from nonhuman primate viruses, pigs are being considered as the choice "donor" animals for xenotransplants. However, pig retroviruses have infected human kidney cells in vitro; and virologists believe that many pig viruses have not been adequately studied. Viruses that are harmless to their animal hosts can be deadly when transmitted to humans. For example, Macaque herpes is harmless to Macaque monkeys, but lethal to humans. The deadly human influenza virus of 1918 that killed more than 20 million people worldwide was a mutation of a swine flu virus that evolved from American pigs and was spread around the world by US troops. Leptospirosis (which produces liver and kidney damage), and erysipelas (a skin infection), are among the approximately 25 known diseases that can be acquired from pigs, all of which could easily affect immunosuppressed humans. There may be myriad unknown "pig diseases" still to be discovered.

Viruses that are harmless to their animal hosts can be deadly when transmitted to humans.

In addition, physiological and anatomical differences between humans and pigs call into question the rationale for their use. These include differences in life-span, heart rate, blood pressure, metabolism, immunology, and regulatory hormones. A pig heart put into a human will turn black and stop beating in fifteen minutes. There is no clinical evidence to suggest that this acute cellular and vascular rejection will ever be overcome, or that organs from genetically bred pigs are any less likely to be rejected by the human body than those from conventional pigs. Moreover, the massive doses of immunosuppressive drugs that would be required for such an operation would likely cause severe toxicity, and increase the patient's chances of developing cancer.

Xenotransplantation gives animal viruses easy access to humans. Transplanting living animal organs into humans circumvents the natural barriers (such as skin and gastrointestinal tract) that prevent infection, thereby facilitating the transmission of infectious diseases from animals to humans.

Unknown factors

No way to screen for unknown viruses. There is no way to screen for unknown viruses. Proceeding with xenotransplantation could expose patients and non-patients to a host of new animal viruses which could remain dormant for months or years before being detected.

Many viruses, as innocuous as the common cold or as lethal as Ebola, can be transmitted via a mere cough or sneeze. An animal virus residing in a xenograft recipient might become airborne, infecting scores of people, and causing a potentially deadly viral epidemic of global proportions akin to HIV or worse. It is highly unlikely that scientists and health care workers would be prepared to cope with such a scenario.

An animal virus residing in a xenograft recipient might become airborne, infecting scores of people, and causing a potentially deadly viral epidemic of global proportions akin to HIV or worse.

Unanswered medico-legal questions. Would the US government be prepared to compensate victims of xenogeneic infections (such as people who may inadvertently contract an infection from a xenograft recipient)? The French government was forced to establish a $2.2 billion fund to compensate victims of AIDS-contaminated blood transfusions administered between 1980 and 1985. Compensation claims in the US have been filed by Persian Gulf War veterans, victims of secret government-sanctioned radiation and syphilis experiments, Vietnam war veterans exposed to Agent Orange, and parents of vaccine-damaged children. The government may now also be held liable for failing to protect citizens from SV40-contaminated polio vaccine. And what about patients who may choose to participate in privately-funded research where there are no mechanisms of accountability to federal health authorities, and little chance (for patients and non-patients) of receiving remuneration for injury or death. Can we afford another public health catastrophe?

The myth of the "germ-free" animal. Xenotransplant proponents claim that they will breed "germ-free" animals to diminish the risk of viral transmission. But in its June 1996 report, the Institute of Medicine acknowledged that "it is not possible to have completely pathogen-free animals, even those derived by Cesarean section, because some potentially infectious agents are passed in the genome and others may be passed transplacentally." Some British virologists say that it would be "a daunting task to eliminate infectious retroviruses from pigs to be used for xenotransplantation, given that [they] estimate approximately 50 PERV [pig endogenous retroviruses] per pig genome."

Weak regulatory oversight, and human error and negligence, would facilitate disease transmission. Proposed regulatory oversight of xenotransplantation procedures is weak and would likely be highly flawed. Virologist Jonathan Allan has stated that, "in choosing voluntary guidelines to be enforced at a local level [via local institutional review boards], . . . the FDA/CDC [Food and Drug Administration/Centers for Disease Control] committee has chosen the least stringent and possibly least successful method of policing these transplant procedures."

Moreover, in all areas of human activity, particularly when money is involved, the potential for fraud, error, and negligence exists. In the past, such behavior has placed human health at considerable risk. Witness the HIV-contaminated blood scandals in France, China, Japan, and the US, for example, in which employees and/or medical authorities knowingly allowed HIV-contaminated blood to be used for transfusions and blood-clotting treatments for hemophiliacs.

Given the enormous amount of data, paperwork, and filing xenotransplant procedures would generate, it would be naive (given human nature) to assume that data will be properly recorded, stored, reviewed, and updated. Regulatory mechanisms often fail to prevent or correct these errors and/or behaviors, the consequences of which could be disastrous in the face of a xenogeneic infection.

The environmental problems posed by xenotransplantation. Breeding animals for xenotransplantation would create a host of environmental problems (including soil and groundwater contamination) associated with the disposal of animal waste, and the carcasses of genetically modified animals and their offspring. Conventional farming and rendering operations have yet to solve these problems which continue to threaten public health across the US.

Emphasizing alternatives

Eating pigs fuels demand for pig organs. Ironically, it is precisely because people eat too many pigs (and other factory-farmed animals), and have unhealthy lifestyles, that pig organ transplants are being considered. A large majority of heart, liver, and kidney transplants could be prevented if people reduced their meat, alcohol, and tobacco consumption. Federal health authorities should be encouraging Americans to take responsibility for their health by eating properly, exercising, and avoiding cigarettes and alcohol.

We should be investing in alternatives to xenotransplantation. Before allocating US funds to such an extreme technology as xenotransplantation, federal public health agencies have a duty to explore proven, less costly, and less risky alternatives. These include 1) preventive health and health maintenance programs aimed at reducing the need for transplants of all kinds, 2) administrative programs to increase human organ donations, 3) clinical research aimed at improving allotransplant technology [transplants between members of the same species], and 4) technologies which lessen our dependence on animals.

Breeding animals for xenotransplantation would create a host of environmental problems . . . associated with the disposal of animal waste, and the carcasses of genetically modified animals and their offspring.

Lifestyle changes can reverse heart disease. Thirteen billion dollars in medical costs could be saved and 100,000 first-time heart attacks averted by the year 2005 if Americans simply reduced their average saturated fat intake by 3 percentage points.

Launching government-funded education campaigns aimed at increasing the pool of human organs should be considered. Neither the government nor the medical community have aggressively encouraged human organ donation. Currently, only 20% of those individuals who die "healthy" have arranged to donate their organs, even though 85% of the public supports organ donation.

Organ availability quadrupled in Austria when its "presumed consent" law was enacted, and similar results prevail in other European countries. The law assumes that everyone is an organ donor unless they specify otherwise. If presumed consent legislation were enacted in the US, 75% of the adult US population (210,000,000) might become committed potential organ donors. Another approach involves creating a legal system of financial incentives to increase organ donation.

Finally, we could be investing in surgical techniques to repair malformed or poorly functioning organs. About 75% of patients who undergo a procedure called ventricular remodeling—in which a section of heart muscle is removed and reshaped—can be taken off the transplant waiting list.

A policy of restraint and humility

Xenotransplantation places public health at substantial risk and hence is an unacceptable technology. Given our society's poor track record in managing the consequences of modern science and technology, including the increasing lethality of military weapons, environmental pollution, rainforest destruction, exponential population growth, and AIDS, we must honestly ask ourselves whether we have the wisdom and moral maturity needed to deal with the consequences of xenotransplantation and related genetic technologies. Until that question is publicly debated and, if ever, answered, logic dictates a policy of restraint and humility. In light of epidemiological, public health, medical, scientific, economic, and environmental issues surrounding xenotransplantation, the Medical Research Modernization Committee advocates an indefinite freeze on all forms of experimentation and clinical application of the technology.

14

Product Testing on Animals Is Cruel and Unnecessary

People for the Ethical Treatment of Animals

People for the Ethical Treatment of Animals (PETA) is the largest animal rights organization in the world. Founded in 1980, PETA is dedicated to establishing and protecting the rights of all animals. PETA operates under the simple principle that animals do not belong to humans to eat, wear, experiment on, or use for entertainment.

A range of household products including cosmetics and cleaners are routinely tested on animals to determine how safe the products are for human use. Some of these animals are subjected to pain in tests of skin or eye irritancy; others are killed while establishing the lethal dose of chemical products. There is no law that requires animal testing to certify product safety, and some companies have abandoned the practice. Yet millions of animals are still suffering and dying in product laboratories all across the nation. Consumers should boycott companies that continue to perpetrate this type of cruelty on animals.

Every year, millions of animals suffer and die in painful tests to determine the "safety" of cosmetics and household products. Substances ranging from eye shadow and soap to furniture polish and oven cleaner are tested on rabbits, rats, guinea pigs, and other animals, despite the fact that test results do not help prevent or treat human illness or injury.

Eye irritancy tests

In these tests, a liquid, flake, granule, or powdered substance is dropped into the eyes of a group of albino rabbits. The animals are often immobilized in stocks from which only their heads protrude. They usually receive no anesthesia during the tests.

After placing the substance in the rabbits' eyes, laboratory technicians record the damage to the eye tissue at specific intervals over an average period of 72 hours, with tests sometimes lasting 7 to 18 days. Reactions to the substances include swollen eyelids, inflamed irises, ulceration, bleeding, massive deterioration, and blindness. During the tests, the rabbits' eyelids are held open with clips. Animals may break their necks as they struggle to escape.

The results of eye irritancy tests are questionable, as they vary from laboratory to laboratory, and even from rabbit to rabbit.

Acute toxicity tests

Acute toxicity tests, commonly called lethal dose or poisoning tests, determine the amount of a substance that will kill a percentage, even up to 100 percent, of a group of test animals.

In these tests, a substance is forced by tube into the animals' stomachs or through holes cut into their throats. It may also be injected under the skin, into a vein, or into the lining of the abdomen; mixed into lab chow; inhaled through a gas mask; or introduced into the eyes, rectum, or vagina. Experimenters observe the animals' reactions, which can include convulsions, labored breathing, diarrhea, constipation, emaciation, skin eruptions, abnormal posture, and bleeding from the eyes, nose, or mouth.[1]

The widely used lethal dose 50 (LD50) test was developed in 1927. The LD50 testing period continues until at least 50 percent of the animals die, usually in two to four weeks.

Like eye irritancy tests, lethal dose tests are unreliable at best. Says Microbiological Associates' Rodger D. Curren, researchers looking for non-animal alternatives must prove that these in vitro models perform "at least as well as animal tests. But as we conduct these validation exercises, it's become more apparent that the animal tests themselves are highly variable."[2] The European Center for the Validation of Alternative Methods' Dr. Michael Ball puts it more strongly: "The scientific basis" for animal safety tests is "weak."[3]

Lethal but legal

No law requires animal testing for cosmetics and household products. The Food and Drug Administration (FDA) requires only that each ingredient in a cosmetics product be "adequately substantiated for safety" prior to marketing or that the product carry a warning label indicating that its safety has not been determined. The FDA does not have the authority to require any particular product test. Likewise, household products, which are regulated by the Consumer Product Safety Commission (CPSC), the agency that administers the Federal Hazardous Substances Act (FHSA), do not have to be tested on animals. A summary of the CPSC's animal-testing policy, printed in the Federal Register, states, "[I]t is important to keep in mind that neither the FHSA nor the Commission's regulations require any firm to perform animal tests. The statute and its implementing regulations only require that a product be labeled to reflect the hazards associated with that product."[4]

Testing methods, therefore, are determined by manufacturers. The very unreliability of animal tests may make them appealing to some companies, since these tests allow manufacturers to put virtually any product on the market. Companies can also use the fact that their products were tested to help defend themselves against consumer lawsuits. Others believe that testing on animals helps them compete in the marketplace: Consumers demand products with exciting new ingredients, such as alpha-hydroxy acids, and animal tests are often considered the easiest and cheapest way to "prove" that new ingredients are "safe."

Alternatives to animal tests

Such arguments carry little weight with the more than 500 manufacturers of cosmetics and household products that have shunned animal tests. These companies take advantage of the many alternatives available today, including cell cultures, tissue cultures, corneas from eye banks, and sophisticated computer and mathematical models. Companies can also formulate products using ingredients already determined to be safe by the FDA. Most cruelty-free companies use a combination of methods to ensure safety, such as maintaining extensive databases of ingredient and formula information and employing in vitro tests and human clinical studies.

A survey by the American Medical Association found that 75 percent of Americans are against using animals to test cosmetics.

Tom's of Maine went one step further. For seven years, the cruelty-free company petitioned the American Dental Association (ADA) to grant its seal of approval to Tom's of Maine toothpastes. Other toothpaste companies unquestioningly conducted lethal tests on rats in order to be eligible for the ADA seal (researchers brush rats' teeth for more than a month, then kill the animals and examine their teeth under a microscope). But Tom's of Maine worked with researchers to develop fluoride tests that could safely be conducted on human volunteers. The ADA finally accepted the results of these tests and granted its seal to several of the company's toothpastes in 1995.[5] The groundbreaking effort by Tom's of Maine to find a humane alternative to accepted, but cruel, practices sets a precedent that other manufacturers can follow in the future.

Compassion in action

Caring consumers also play a vital role in eliminating cruel test methods. Spurred by public outrage, the European Union (EU) proposed banning cosmetics tests on animals by 1998; unfortunately, the EU has indefinitely delayed this ban because of complaints by animal-testing companies. But other organizations in Europe have stepped in. For example, after conducting surveys showing that four out of five of its customers are against testing cosmetics and household products on animals, the Co-op, Britain's largest retailer, launched its own campaign urging companies to end such tests. [Britain announced a voluntary ban in November 1998.]

In the United States, a survey by the American Medical Association found that 75 percent of Americans are against using animals to test cosmetics.[6] Hundreds of companies have responded by switching to animal-friendly test methods. To help consumers identify products that are truly cruelty-free, a coalition of national animal protection groups has developed the Corporate Standard of Compassion for Animals, which clarifies the non-animal-testing terminology and procedures used by manufacturers and makes available a cruelty-free logo for companies that are in compliance with the standard. Shoppers can support this initiative by purchasing products that comply with the corporate standard, and boycotting those that don't, and by asking local stores to carry cruelty-free items.

Everyone seeking to stop animal tests should also urge government regulatory agencies and trade associations like the American Dental Association to accept non-animal test methods immediately.

References

1. Rowan, A.N. *Of Mice, Models, & Men: A Critical Evaluation of Animal Research* (Albany: State University of New York Press, 1984).

2. Branna, Tom, "Animal Testing Alternatives: Moving Closer to Validation?" *happi*, February 1995.

3. Ibid.

4. *Federal Register,* Vol. 49, No. 105.

5. Ahrens, Frank, "Why Is This Rat Smiling?" *The Washington Post,* August 17, 1995.

6. Branna.

15

Military Experimentation on Animals Is Inhumane

People for the Ethical Treatment of Animals

People for the Ethical Treatment of Animals (PETA) is the largest animal rights organization in the world. Founded in 1980, PETA is dedicated to establishing and protecting the rights of all animals. PETA operates under the simple principle that animals do not belong to humans to eat, wear, experiment on, or use for entertainment.

The U.S. government uses hundreds of thousands of animals in military experiments every year. These experiments range from studying wounds received from specific weapons to examining the effects of radiation on living tissue in preparation for coping with a nuclear war. All of these tests are extremely cruel and vicious, and the information that is gathered is rarely applicable to humans.

When news reports tally the casualties of war, or when monuments are erected to honor soldiers, the other-than-human victims of war—the animals whose bodies are shot, burned, poisoned, and otherwise tortured in tests to create even more ways to kill people—are never recognized, nor is their suffering well known. The 1987 movie "Project X" offered only a glimpse of the kind of experiments that go on far from public view but at taxpayer expense.

Uncounted casualties

The U.S. military inflicts the pains of war on hundreds of thousands of animals each year in experiments. The Department of Defense (DOD) and the Veterans Administration (VA) together are the federal government's second largest user of animals (after the National Institutes of Health). They account for nearly half the estimated minimum of 1.6 million dogs, cats, guinea pigs, hamsters, rabbits, primates, rats, mice, and "wild animals" used, as reported to Congress in 1983, the last year for which government figures are available.[1] Because these figures don't include exper-

Reprinted, with permission, from "Military Testing: The Unseen War," a factsheet from the People for the Ethical Treatment of Animals website: www.peta-online.org/facts/exp/fsexp09.htm.

iments that were contracted out to non-governmental laboratories, or the many sheep, goats, and pigs often shot in wound experiments, the actual total of animal victims is probably much higher.

The House Armed Services Committee voiced its concern "about the use of animals in medical and other defense-related research" in its report on the National Defense Authorization Act for fiscal year 1995.[2] At committee hearings, DOD revealed that its use of animals in experiments has increased 36% in the past decade, but that it spent $180 million on research using 553,000 animals in the last fiscal year.[3]

Top Secret

Military testing is classified "Top Secret," and it is very hard to get current information. From published research, we know that armed forces facilities all over the United States test all manner of weaponry on animals, from Soviet AK-47 rifles to biological and chemical warfare agents to nuclear blasts. Military experiments can be acutely painful, repetitive, costly, and unreliable, and they are particularly wasteful because most of the effects they study can be, or have already been, observed in humans, or the results cannot be extrapolated to human experience.

Sample experiments

Burns and Blasts: In 1946, near the Bikini Atoll in the South Pacific, 4,000 sheep, goats, and other animals loaded onto a boat and set adrift were killed or severely burned by an atomic blast detonated above them. The military nicknamed the experiment "The Atomic Ark."[4]

At the Army's Fort Sam Houston, live rats were immersed in boiling water for 10 seconds, and a group of them were then infected on parts of their burned bodies.[5]

In 1987, at the Naval Medical Institute in Maryland, rats' backs were shaved, covered with ethanol, and then "flamed" for 10 seconds.[6]

In 1988, at Kirkland Air Force Base in New Mexico, sheep were placed in a loose net sling against a reflecting plate, and an explosive device was detonated 19 meters away. In two of the experiments, 48 sheep were blasted: the first group to test the value of a vest worn during the blast, and the second to see if chemical markers aided in the diagnosis of blast injury (they did not).[7]

> *From published research, we know that armed forces facilities all over the United States test all manner of weaponry on animals, from Soviet AK-47 rifles to biological and chemical warfare agents to nuclear blasts.*

Radiation: At the Armed Forces Radiobiology Research Institute in Maryland, nine rhesus monkeys were strapped in chairs and exposed to total-body irradiation. Within two hours, six of the nine were vomiting, hypersalivating, and chewing.[8] In another experiment, 17 beagles were exposed to total-body irradiation, studied for one to seven days, and then killed. The experimenter concluded that radiation affects the gallbladder.[9]

At Brooks Air Force Base in Texas, rhesus monkeys were strapped to a B52 flight simulator (the "Primate Equilibrium Platform"). After being prodded with painful electric shocks to learn to "fly" the device, the monkeys were irradiated with gamma rays to see if they could hold out "for the 10 hours it would take to bomb an imaginary Moscow." Those hit with the heaviest doses vomited violently and became extremely lethargic before being killed.[10]

Diseases: To evaluate the effect of temperature on the transmission of the Dengue 2 virus, a mosquito-transmitted disease that causes fever, muscle pain, and rash, experiments conducted by the U.S. Army at Fort Detrick, Md., involved shaving the stomachs of adult rhesus monkeys and then attaching cartons of mosquitoes to their bodies to allow the mosquitoes to feed.[11]

Experimenters at Fort Detrick have also invented a rabbit restraining device that consists of a small cage that pins the rabbits down with steel rods while mosquitoes feast on their bodies.[12]

Wound Labs: The Department of Defense has operated "wound labs" since 1957. At these sites, conscious or semiconscious animals are suspended from slings and shot with high-powered weapons to inflict battlelike injuries for military surgical practice. In 1983, in response to public pressure, Congress limited the use of dogs in these labs, but countless goats, pigs, and sheep are still being shot, and at least one laboratory continues to shoot cats. At the Army's Fort Sam Houston "Goat Lab," goats are hung upside down and shot in their hind legs. After physicians practice excising the wounds, any goat who survives is killed.[13]

Other forms of military experiments include subjecting animals to decompression sickness, weightlessness, drugs and alcohol, smoke inhalation, and pure oxygen inhalation.

Animal intelligence

The Armed Forces conscript various animals into intelligence and combat service, sending them on "missions" that endanger their lives and well-being. The Marine Corps teaches dogs "mauling, snarling, sniffing, and other suitable skills" needed to search for bombs and drugs.[14] Additionally, thousands of rabbits, chickens, and goats are bludgeoned, strangled, or decapitated every year in military "food procurement exercises" as part of survival skills training at bases across the country.

Thousands of animals also fall victim to military operations and even military fashion. A series of Navy tests of underwater explosives in the Chesapeake Bay in 1987 killed more than 3,000 fish,[15] and habitats for hundreds of species have been destroyed by nuclear tests in the South Pacific and the American Southwest.

And as if weapons tests didn't kill enough animals, the Air Force recently awarded a New Jersey company $5.2 million to manufacture 53,000 leather flight jackets, in an effort to "enhance esprit" among its pilots. At 3½ goat skins per jacket, the result will be that 185,500 African goats will lose their lives so that U.S. pilots can sport a World War II "look."[16]

References

1. "Alternatives to Animal Use in Research, Testing, and Education," U.S. Office of Technology Assessment, 1986, pp. 50–51.

2. Krizmanic, Judy, "Military Increases Animal Experiments," *Vegetarian Times*, August 1994.

3. Ibid.

4. Tom Regan, "We Are All Noah," 1985.

5. Burleson, "Flow Cytometric Measurement of Rat Lymphocite Subpopulations After Burn Injury and Injury With Infection," *Archives of Surgery*, 122:216.

6. Wretland, et al., "Role of Exotoxin A and Elastase in the Pseudomonas Aeruginosa Strain PAO Experimental Mouse Burn Infection," *Microbial Pathogenesis*, 2:397, 1987.

7. Phillips, et al., "Cloth Ballistic Vest Alters Response to Blast," *Journal of Trauma*, January 28, 1988.

8. Dubas, et al., "Effect of Ionizing Radiation on Prostaglandins and Gastric Secretion in Rhesus Monkeys," *Radiation Research*, 110:289, 1987.

9. Durakovic, "Hepatobiliary Kinetics After Whole Body Irradiation," *Military Medicine*, 151(9):487.

10. "Obscure Office Drafts World War III Script," *Washington Post*, May 27, 1984.

11. Watts, et al., "Effect of Temperature on the Vector Efficiency of Aedes Aegypti for Dengue 2 Virus," *American Journal of Tropical Medicine and Hygiene*, 36(1):143, 1987.

12. Dobson, et al., "A Device for Restraining Rabbits While Bloodfeeding Mosquitoes," *Laboratory Animal Science*, 37(3):364, 1987.

13. "Goats Shot to Teach Army Doctors Skills," *Williamsport Sun-Gazette*, March 5, 1986.

14. "Uncle Sam Wants You, Too, Fido," *Time*, June 18, 1984, p. 33.

15. "Fish Deaths Cancel Navy Blast Tests," *Washington Post*, October 1, 1987.

16. "Air Force Needs a Few Goat Jackets," *San Francisco Chronicle*, April 8, 1988.

16

Animal Experimentation in Education Is Unethical

Katherine Lewis

Katherine Lewis is the director of education for the American Anti-Vivisection Society (AAVS), and a contributor to AV Magazine, *the organization's publication. The AAVS is devoted to ending animal experimentation.*

By making animal dissection part of academic curricula, the education system is molding students to view animal experimentation as ethically acceptable. Instead, students should be encouraged to express freedom of choice concerning their participation in animal dissection. Furthermore, most students will never make use of animal experimentation in their future occupations, and therefore should not be compelled to take part in course work that may conflict with their ethical beliefs.

Education is a process of training and/or developing knowledge. Ethics is the system, or code of morals, that a particular person, religion, or group holds. To speak of animals, ethics and education, we must explore the relationship between animals, the process of educating our young adults and the moral standards of our students, parents and educators.

To clarify the relationship, we need to closely examine education as a process of training and developing knowledge. What sort of knowledge is being imparted? For many, this training and knowledge gathering involves learning about various subjects. This training is also involved in the creation of the next generation—molding our next set of citizens. For this purpose, schools often serve to perpetuate "the logic of the present system and bring conformity to it." However, schools also can provide an opportunity for "'the practice of freedom,' the means by which women and men (girls and boys) deal critically and creatively with reality and discover how to participate in the transformation of their world" (Friere, 1968).

This "practice of freedom" is integral to creating ethical education that frees students to look critically and creatively at systems and individuals who perpetuate the abuses of our world and its inhabitants. In

Reprinted from Katherine Lewis, "Animals, Ethics, and Education," *AV Magazine*, Winter 1998, with permission.

most of our current education, we, as a society, deny the interconnection that students feel with the world and its inhabitants.

The current system of science education does not allow the student the "practice of freedom." Science, as it is taught today, alienates students from the natural world, teaching that animals are something to dissect in a lab rather than to observe in their habitat. Through attempts to provide students with scientific reason and the promotion of certain activities, educators foster the idea that humans have the right to do with other species as we wish for the purposes of education. This has dramatic ethical ramifications for the students who are being taught.

> *Science, as it is taught today, alienates students from the natural world, teaching that animals are something to dissect in a lab rather than to observe in their habitat.*

The *Journal of Contemporary Ethnography* published an article called "Learning the Scientist's Role: Animal Dissection in Middle School," in which Dorian Solot and Arnold Arluke discuss the transformation that occurs with middle-school students dealing with the dissection of fetal pigs. They discuss the coping skills that are used to deal with this dissection and they argue "that dissection in middle-school science class indoctrinates American children into the cultural understanding of science and its perspective toward the use of animals." They go on to state that "(s)chools after all, are the vital sites of mass socialization; embedded in curricula are societal beliefs, values, attitudes and moral codes." They continue to identify coping strategies that students go through and state that "schools socialize students to reproduce the perspective of modern Western science and the kind of human animal relationship it implies" (Solot and Arluke, 1997).

Hundreds of thousands of young adults in junior and senior high schools, colleges and universities are asked to dissect animals in their Biology, Advanced Placement Biology and Anatomy and Physiology courses every year. Even though statistics show that out of every 1,000 students entering the fifth grade, only 220 will graduate from college and only 40 will obtain science degrees, almost all 1,000 will dissect an animal before they leave high school. Of those 40 who receive their degrees in science, very few will enter a field where dissection experience is even remotely related. For those students who are interested in the medical field before they dissect, the idea of taking a life and learning they will be forced to take more lives as their schooling continues, is so disturbing that many rethink the idea completely. For students in junior and senior high school and college, the dissection of a once living being is not only unethical, but unnecessary.

Forcing an unnatural attitude

When students are socialized to reproduce the current and pervasive scientific model, they are pressured to deny their innate connection with the world and its inhabitants. They are persuaded to examine animals as expendable objects who serve as education tools, not as living, feeling beings. When students are forced to dissect animals such as frogs and cats, they must divorce themselves from their innate humane feeling for these animals (Solot and Arluke, 1997).

In science classes, children are taught to dissect a once living animal to study comparative anatomy, not to consider the ethics of the dissection of once living animals. The ethics of taking a life, whether it be a cat or a frog, for the purpose of teaching, is irrefutably ethically questionable. And yet, this ethical dilemma is often overlooked. Why? Is it because educators do not want students to examine the deeper moral and ethical questions that this presents—do they want to maintain the "status quo?" Or is it because some educators themselves have failed to examine these ethical questions? Whatever the reason, it provides potential tension within the classroom. When a student confronts and even challenges the ethics and tradition of an educator, she/he forces the issue of the ethical treatment of animals into the limelight of the classroom. Every year, thousands of students do exactly this. Whether it be a student in a middle school who calls Animalearn because she objects to a guinea pig experiment, a high school student who won't do an essay regarding the benefits and advances of biomedical research instead choosing to do an essay on alternatives to animal experimentation, or a college student who refuses to dissect a cat, students are acting as our agents of moral change.

So what can be done to assist our young people? We must educate our educators. These young people are doing an excellent job, but we as citizens and animal advocates must also take the opportunity to awaken educators to their biases and their preoccupation with the perpetuation of the past. We must let them learn by example. Let them know that Switzerland, Norway, India, Argentina, the Netherlands, Slovakia and Denmark have all prohibited dissection below the university level.

Education should foster compassion and respect for life, rather than devalue life and promote the notion that animals are expendable. According to moral development theorists, people beyond the age of thirteen are able to perceive that what is right is determined by universal principles of justice, reciprocity and equality. The actions of the individual are based on a combination of conscience and these ethical principles. It is clear that the students are ready to embrace ethics, justice and compassion—rather than devaluing life. Let's all contribute to assisting our students in becoming critical, creative and compassionate citizens—creating a harmony between animals, ethics and education.

Bibliography

Freire, P. 1968. *Pedagogy of the Oppressed*. New York. Seabury Press.

Morrison, G. 1991. *Early Childhood Education Today*. New York. Macmillan Publishing Company.

Solot, D. and Arnold Arluke, "Learning the Scientist's Role: Animal Dissection in Middle School." *Journal of Contemporary Ethnography*. Vol. 26 No. 1, April 1997.

17

Alternatives to Animal Testing Should Be Pursued

Leslie Pardue

Leslie Pardue is a writer who has published articles in E Magazine, *an environmental journal.*

Although some environmental scientists rely on data gathered from animal testing, many of these researchers agree with animal welfare advocates who suggest that such tests can be replaced with nonanimal alternatives. Alternative models are often cheaper and more accurate than animal testing. Unfortunately, seeking alternatives has not been prioritized in research fields because animal testing is routine and scientists are not often asked to reexamine their research methods.

To an outsider, environmentalists and animal rights advocates would appear natural allies. But one basic philosophical difference divides the two schools of thought: to the extent that environmental organizations work on animal issues, they tend to emphasize the health and viability of animal species, populations and habitat; animal rights advocates, on the other hand, concern themselves more with the well-being of individual animals and work on issues dealing with individual animal suffering and pain.

While many people would place themselves squarely in both camps, arguing that concern for the welfare of individual animals is inseparable from environmental concerns, many environmental organizations prefer to distance themselves from animal rights groups which they view as misanthropic, tunnel-visioned, sensational in approach, and anti-science.

Portraying animal rights advocacy as "shrieking," "a religion" and "a one-note samba," Margaret L. Knox, writing in the May/June 1991 issue of *Buzzworm*, warns environmentalists to not allow their message to be diluted by the animal rights viewpoint, "lest the ever-elusive big picture doesn't get miniaturized into portraits of battered puppy dogs." In the April/May 1993 issue of *Garbage*, Bill Breen does little to tone down the rhetoric. Articulating the mainstream view, he labels as "terrorist" the

Reprinted, with permission, from Leslie Pardue, "Testing for Toxins: Environmental and Humane Groups Seek Alternatives to Animal Tests," *E/The Environmental Magazine*, February 1, 1994. Subscription Department: PO Box 2047, Marion, OH 43306; Telephone: (815) 734-1242. Subscriptions are $20 per year.

clandestine Animal Liberation Front (ALF) (which has raided and vandalized animal testing laboratories to call attention to their concerns), while pointing out that a host of current environmental laws—the Clean Air and Water Act, Superfund legislation and many Environmental Protection Agency (EPA) regulations—were in fact formulated using animal test data. While acknowledging that some animal tests, such as the Lethal Dose 50 Percent (LD50) and the Maximum Tolerated Dose (MTD), may yield results that are statistically invalid and difficult to extrapolate to humans, he nevertheless concludes, "Though imperfect, in most tests the mouse remains the best model for man."

Advocating alternatives

Dr. Kenneth Olden is director of the National Institute of Environmental Health Sciences which direct animal toxicology studies for the federal government. In a March 23, 1993, *New York Times* article ("Animal Tests As Risk Clues: The Best Data May Fall Short"), Dr. Olden questions the billions of dollars spent each year regulating chemicals that may pose little health or environmental risk. Indeed, scientists are questioning regulations governing such chemicals as dioxin, DDT, saccharin and cyclamates, which have produced cancers in some lab animal tests but may not be as harmful to humans. Institute officials estimate that between one-third and two-thirds of substances deemed to be carcinogenic as a result of MTD tests in rodents would be benign in humans at normal doses. "Quite often," reports the *Times*, "that means no one takes the Institute's warnings seriously anymore." A panel appointed by Olden concluded that, rather than relying solely on animal test data to determine health risks to humans, government should redirect its efforts toward cell cultures and epidemiological studies on human populations that have accidentally experienced chemical exposure.

> *Although not all animal welfare organizations favor the abolition of animal testing, most agree that many such tests could—and should—be replaced by alternative techniques.*

Although not all animal welfare organizations favor the abolition of animal testing, most agree that many such tests could—and should—be replaced by alternative techniques. "*Animal* tests have a host of problems besides animal suffering associated with them," says Dr. Martin Stephens of the Humane Society of the United States (HSUS). "They're expensive, time consuming and often have dubious applicability to humans. There are so many species to test on, and so many doses that can be administered, that scientists can theoretically come up with whatever results they're looking for." Many alternatives, he argues, are often quicker, cheaper and more accurate.

Environmental organizations currently rely on data from animal tests when trying to prove a chemical to be harmful to the environment. But Stephens points to Corrosistex, which chemically assesses the toxicity of often-transported chemicals; Fetek, which uses tadpoles instead of rodents to measure fetal abnormalities; and TopKat, a computer program that assesses toxicity based upon comparisons with hundreds of other already-tested chemicals. "Scientists should avail themselves of such alternatives and environmentalists should see that more are developed," says Stephens.

However, many alternatives have not yet been validated by the scientific community. Animal advocate Henry Spira interviewed in the newsletter of the Foundation for Biomedical Research (FBR), comments, "A lot of the block have nothing to do with science but with regulatory requirements and bureaucratic inertia . . . there comes a point where you have to stop designing and start shipping."

Reexamining current methods

Toward that end, Spira advocates challenging "creeping routinism." "Institutions should be called upon to examine animal research activities from ground zero, so that people do not mindlessly repeat what was done in previous years. . . . People and institutions tend to do tomorrow what they did yesterday," argues Spira. "Before any laboratory animals are used we must ask, 'Is this research really necessary? Can this information be obtained without using animals? With fewer animals? With less pain?'" Spira advocates the adoption of the "Three Rs": replacement of animal tests, reduction in the numbers of animals used (currently some 20 million annually in the U.S.), and refinement of experimental procedures so as to lessen animal suffering.

Although most scientists feel that alternative testing methods won't ever fully replace the use of animals, "The animal welfare community has done an extraordinary service to science in challenging all of us to examine research protocols more strenuously," says Ellen Silbergeld, a toxicologist with the Environmental Defense Fund. "An animal rights viewpoint is essential to modern environmental and ethical thinking and behavior," agrees Dr. Peter Montague of the Environmental Research Foundation. "At present, animal testing is necessary for assessing the toxicity of chemicals . . . [but] this does not imply that treatment of animals cannot be improved." Montague advocates the principle of "precautionary action," by which "evidence of harm to animals would result in an active program to remove the offending chemical from commerce, in which case no further testing would be necessary." Says Silbergeld, "Environmentalists and animal rights activists can work together to insist on a minimum set of data relevant to making decisions—and once that data is obtained, that's it. To do it again is bad science, bad policy and bad ethics."

18

Perspectives on Alternatives to Animal Testing

Kathryn Rogers

Kathryn Rogers is the religion writer for the St. Louis Post-Dispatch.

Despite agreement that alternatives to animal experimentation should be examined and tested, advocates for and against the use of animals in research differ on the feasibility of ending all animal experimentation. Those who favor abolishing animal testing state that it is irrelevant and inhumane. Those who see no end to animal testing stipulate that animal models are still the most useful because the complexity of living organisms cannot be replicated by other means.

William J. Longmore and Sammy Shoss represent two sides of a long-standing dispute that shows no sign of resolution. Two decades after the animal rights movement heated up in this country and three decades after the Animal Welfare Act was passed, animal rights activists and medical researchers remain stubborn opponents.

Ironically, the two sides agree on the principle at the heart of the fray: Both researchers and animal rights groups say they want research on animals to end.

But scientists won't stop using the animals until alternative methods as effective as animal research are available, they say. And many don't believe that will ever happen. The National Institutes of Health has allocated $12.7 billion for research this year. In 40 percent of the projects, some animals are used, officials say.

Researchers put the number of animals used nationwide at about 18 million a year; activists say the number is closer to 70 million. Rats and mice are most often used. In addition, in 1995—the last year for which figures are available, about 1.4 million dogs, cats, primates, guinea pigs, hamsters and rabbits were used in publicly funded research.

Some procedures permitted on animals for research purposes include surgery on the brain, spinal chord and all organs; transplants of organs from one animal to another, even from one species to another; injury to

81

the head to study brain trauma; the breaking of bones and cutting of the spinal chord; induction of diseases and conditions of all kinds, including nicotine and heroin addiction; and mild electric shock.

Anesthesia and analgesics are required in most cases, but pain may be induced without anesthesia or painkiller in certain circumstances, such as in the study of pain itself.

"Animal models help us understand and treat human disorder," says Dr. Theodore Cicero, vice chancellor of research and vice chancellor of animal affairs at Washington University School of Medicine. "We are not evil people. . . . We're trying to do good for mankind."

Like others in research, Cicero and Longmore deny claims by activists that nonanimal alternatives—such as synthetic cell cultures, human tissue cultures and computer technology—make using animals obsolete.

These research methods are helpful and are used when possible, Cicero says, but while they can simplify procedures, "none will predict what's going to happen in a complex living organism."

Longmore's research was aimed at respiratory problems in premature infants. The study showed that these infants' lungs lacked an adequate amount of a substance called pulmonary surfactant, which allows the lungs to fill up with air again easily after exhaling. The infants had to struggle to breathe, he said.

His work, along with work elsewhere in the country and Japan, led to the development of a product called Survanta, which is made from cow lung. It is now used widely to treat infants with the disorder.

"I feel lucky to be involved in science that has had such a direct benefit," Longmore says. Now, he is involved with similar research on respiratory disorders caused by lung injury.

Longmore admits that feelings about animals can pose a dilemma in research. He said that a few years ago, he tried to work on ferrets but had to give it up.

"They make eye contact," he said. "And they're really lovable animals."

Longmore and others say the Animal Welfare Act and other government regulations, as well as the research institutions' own rules, protect animals from unnecessary suffering. But animal-rights activists say policing of research institutions for compliance with law is inadequate: In 1995, for instance, the U.S. Department of Agriculture had 69 inspectors to check 2,688 research sites.

A paradigm shift

Even if the rules are followed, activists say, much animal research is repetitive, irrelevant or cruel. They cite projects that tend to make the listener cringe: gunshot wounds in cats, crack-cocaine addiction in monkeys.

And not all medical people agree that animals are necessary in research. Dr. Neal Barnard, a psychiatrist and president of the Physicians Committee for Responsible Medicine, said experiments on animals had produced misleading results on strokes, polio, lung cancer, birth defects and various drugs, sometimes to the detriment of humans. Barnard conducts nutrition research and has written books on nutrition. His group claims nearly 5,000 physician members and 80,000 nonphysician members.

"We've got to get it out of our heads that there is a cure for AIDS right around the corner if we just use another animal or two," Barnard said. "If we're going to find answers to human problems, we have to look at human beings in ways we never have before."

Barnard says good epidemiological studies can tell us much about human disease prevention and treatment that animal research can not.

Medical researchers argue that animal experiments have been crucial to the development of such things as antibiotics, hypertension treatment, organ transplantation and open-heart surgery. They also say they would not use animals if they didn't have to.

"Our own sensibilities about using animals and causing pain and distress to a living organism is distasteful to most of us," Cicero said.

Despite those concerns, funding nationally for studies into the development of nonanimal research alternatives is tiny compared to the amount going into general research. The National Institute of Environmental Health Sciences awards $1.5 million a year for studies that look for research alternatives, only some of which don't use animals at all. Some of the alternatives use fewer animals or species lower than mammals.

Scientists won't stop using . . . animals until alternative methods as effective as animal research are available. . . . And many don't believe that will ever happen.

The institute is the only one formally studying alternatives. It says that all its research into test validation—$30 million worth—indirectly looks at animal research.

In 1997, the Center for Alternatives to Animal Testing at Johns Hopkins University is funding 11 projects at $20,000 apiece. Only some of those projects use no animals at all.

Joanne Zurlo, associate director, says scientists are posing "a lot of resistance" to replacing animals in research, partly because animal-rights extremists have pushed them into a defensive, close-the-ranks position and partly because "there needs to be more information on nonanimal models."

But she also attributes the resistance to the fact that "this is a basic shift of a paradigm and like any group, researchers are resistant to a paradigm shift."

Andrew N. Rowan, director of the Tufts University Center for Animals and Public Policy, says medical researchers make exaggerated claims as to the benefits of *animal* experimentation: "They say it saves all those lives, and it's not clear that it does."

But Rowan says animal rights activists are wrong when they assert that animal research has done little for human health. For Rowan, the moral argument against animal research "is far less easily rejected."

A higher value

The moral bottom line for activists in St. Louis and with the national office of People for the Ethical Treatment of Animals (PETA) is the suffering.

"Animals know pain, they know the feeling of fear, they can definitely feel stress," says Jenny Woods, a spokeswoman for PETA. "They are kept in cages in unnatural environments. It's wrong to impose that upon them" no matter what the motives are, she says.

We've got to get it out of our heads that there is a cure for AIDS right around the corner if we just use another animal or two.

Dr. Richard Doyle, a veterinarian and director of the department of comparative medicine at St. Louis University Health Sciences Center, says animals used in experiments are serving "a higher value"—the easing of human suffering.

Woods and other activists counter that the notion that human life is more valuable than animal life is "speciesism." They say researchers would consider it unethical to experiment on severely retarded people or on humans in vegetative states, yet would readily use animals because animals don't have certain intellectual or moral capacities.

But Cicero argues, "Do we have the right as people in the medical profession . . . to not carry out studies in animals even though we know that they will lead to a cure? I don't think we have the right to make that decision."

Shoss, a member of the St. Louis Animal Rights Team, concedes that she was helped by techniques and treatments developed in research that used animals.

But after her illness, "I said to myself, how can one animal be my beloved pet and another be an animal experiment.

"A lot of researchers say it's impossible to not use animals, but we've got to move toward that," says Shoss, a vegetarian who does not consume dairy products or eggs nor use any animal products. "These are sentient beings. They feel the pain. For what little good that may come of it, it's ethically wrong."

Two sides

Sammy Shoss, an animal rights activist from Creve Coeur, came to oppose the use of animals in medical research after she suffered a medical crisis. A heart attack in 1987 was nearly fatal; she was on life support for a week.

"I didn't have an out-of-body experience, there was no light, no tunnels," said Shoss, 61. "But I came to realize that all the education, all the travel I'd done, everything I had didn't matter. The only thing that mattered was my life. And if my life was that valuable to me, then it's that valuable to animals. Life is all that any creature is given."

William J. Longmore, 65, of Warson Woods, is a professor of biochemistry and molecular biology at St. Louis University and has used animals in experiments for years. His research, which used laboratory rats, contributed to the development of a medication to treat premature babies with respiratory distress syndrome.

"I'm a very soft person, but I just don't have a problem with using animals in research that's going to benefit human life," said Longmore, who has had laboratory animals as pets, along with a dachsund. A Presbyterian, Longmore says his belief that human life is more important than animal life "is a religious feeling."

Organizations to Contact

The editors have compiled the following list of organizations concerned with the issues debated in this book. The descriptions are derived from materials provided by the organizations. All have publications or information available for interested readers. The list was compiled on the date of publication of the present volume; the information provided here may change. Be aware that many organizations take several weeks or longer to respond to inquiries, so allow as much time as possible.

American Anti-Vivisection Society (AAVS)
801 Old York Rd., Suite 204, Jenkintown, PA 19046
(215) 887-0816 • fax: (215) 887-2088
website: http://www.aavs.org

AAVS advocates the abolition of vivisection, opposes all types of experiments on living animals, and sponsors research on alternatives to these methods. The society produces videos and publishes numerous brochures, including *Vivisection and Dissection and the Classroom: A Guide to Conscientious Objection*, and the bimonthly *AV Magazine*.

American Association for Laboratory Animal Science (AALAS)
9190 Crestwyn Hills Dr., Memphis, TN 38125
(901) 754-8620 • fax: (901) 759-5849
website: http://www.aalas.org

AALAS is a professional nonprofit association concerned with the production, care, and study of animals used in biomedical research. The association provides a medium for the exchange of scientific information on all phases of laboratory animal care and use through its educational activities, publications, and certification program.

Americans for Medical Progress (AMP)
421 King St., Suite 401, Alexandria, VA 22314
(703) 836-9595 • fax: (703) 836-9594
e-mail: info@amprogress.org • website: http://www.amprogress.org

AMP is a nonprofit organization working to raise public awareness concerning the use of animals in research, in order to ensure that scientists and doctors have the freedom and resources necessary to pursue their research. AMP exposes the misinformation of the animal rights movement through newspaper and magazine articles, broadcast debates, and public education materials.

Animal Alliance of Canada
221 Broadview Ave., Suite 101, Toronto, Ont., CANADA, M4M 2G3
(416) 462-9541 • fax: (416) 462-9647
website: http://www.animalalliance.ca

The Animal Alliance of Canada is an animal rights advocacy and education group that focuses on local, regional, national, and international issues concerning the good will toward and respectful treatment of animals by humans.

The alliance acts through research, investigation, education, advocacy, and legislation. Publications include factsheets, legislative updates, opinion editorials, and the newsletter *TakeAction*.

Animal Welfare Institute (AWI)
PO Box 3650, Washington, DC 20007
(202) 337-2332 • fax: (202) 338-9478
e-mail: awi@animalwelfare.com • website: http://www.animalwelfare.com

Founded in 1951, the AWI is a nonprofit charitable organization working to reduce pain and fear inflicted on animals by humans. AWI believes in the humane treatment of laboratory animals and the development and use of non-animal testing methods, and encourages humane science teaching and prevention of painful experiments on animals by high school students. In addition to publishing *AWI Quarterly*, the institute also offers numerous books, pamphlets, and on-line articles.

Incurably Ill for Animal Research
PO Box 27454, Lansing, MI 48909
(517) 887-1141

This organization consists of people who have incurable diseases and are concerned that the use of animals in medical research will be stopped or severely limited by animal rights activists, thus delaying or preventing the development of new cures. It publishes the monthly *Bulletin* and a quarterly newsletter.

Institute for In Vitro Sciences
21 Firstfield Rd., Suite 220, Gaithersburg, MD 20878
(301) 947-6523 • fax: (301) 947-6538
website: http://www.iivs.org

The institute is a nonprofit technology-driven foundation for the advancement of alternative methods to animal testing. Its mission is to facilitate the replacement of animal testing through the use of *in vitro* technology, conduct *in vitro* testing for industry and government, and provide educational and technical resources to the public and private sectors.

Medical Research Modernization Committee (MRMC)
20145 Van Aken Blvd., #24, Shaker Heights, OH 44122
phone and fax: (216) 283-6702
website: http://www.mrmcmed.org

The MRMC is a national health advocacy group composed of physicians, scientists, and other health care professionals who evaluate the benefits, risks, and costs of medical research methods and technologies. The committee believes that animals are inadequate models for testing medical treatments and that research money would be better spent on human clinical research studies.

National Animal Interest Alliance (NAIA)
PO Box 66579, Portland, OR 97290
(503) 761-1139
e-mail: NAIA@naiaonline.org • website: http://www.naiaonline.org

NAIA is an association of business, agricultural, scientific, and recreational interests formed to protect and promote humane practices and relationships between people and animals. NAIA provides the network necessary for diverse animal rights groups to communicate with one another, to describe the nature and value of their work, to clarify animal rights misinformation, and to educate each other and the public about what they do and how they do it. NAIA serves as a clearinghouse for information and as an access point for subject matter experts, keynote speakers, and issue analysis. The alliance also publishes the bimonthly newspaper *NAIA News*.

The Nature of Wellness
PO Box 10400, Glendale, CA 91209
(818) 790-6384 • fax: (818) 790-9660
website: http://www.animalresearch.org

The Nature of Wellness is a nonprofit organization whose objective is to bring about total abolition of the practice of animal experimentation. The Nature of Wellness informs the public about the medical and scientific invalidity and counterproductiveness of animal experimentation and the massive damage it causes to human health, environment, and economy through print ads and its television documentary *Lethal Medicine*.

People for the Ethical Treatment of Animals (PETA)
501 Front St., Norfolk, VA 23510
(757) 622-7382 • fax: (757) 622-0457
e-mail: peta@norfolk.infini.net • website: http://www.peta-online.org

An international animal rights organization, PETA is dedicated to establishing and protecting the rights of all animals. It focuses on four areas: factory farms, research laboratories, the fur trade, and the entertainment industry. PETA promotes public education, cruelty investigations, animal rescue, celebrity involvement, and legislative action. It produces numerous videos and publishes *Animal Times*, *Grrr!*, various fact sheets, brochures, and flyers.

Physicians Committee for Responsible Medicine (PCRM)
5100 Wisconsin Ave., Suite 404, Washington, DC 20016
(202) 686-2210 • fax: (202) 686-2216
e-mail: pcrm@pcrm.org • website: http://www.pcrm.org

Founded in 1985, PCRM is a nonprofit organization supported by physicians and laypersons to encourage higher standards for ethics and effectiveness in research. It promotes using nonanimal alternatives in both research and education. The committee publishes the quarterly magazine *Good Medicine* and numerous fact sheets on animal experimentation issues.

Psychologists for the Ethical Treatment of Animals (PSYETA)
403 McCauley St., PO Box 1297, Washington Grove, MD 20880
phone and fax: (301) 565-4167
website: http://www.psyeta.org

PSYETA seeks to ensure proper treatment of animals used in psychological research and education and urges revision of curricula to include ethical issues in the treatment of animals. It developed a tool to measure the invasiveness or severity of animal experiments. Its publications include the book *Animal Models of Human Psychology* and the journals *Society and Animals* and *Journal of Applied Animal Welfare Science*.

Seriously Ill for Medical Research
PO Box 504, Dunstable, Bedfordshire, LU6 2LU, United Kingdom
(44) 01582 873108 • fax: (44) 01582 873705
e-mail: SIMR@dircon.co.uk • website: http://www.simr.dircon.co.uk

SIMR is a patients' group formed to voice support for humane research into disabling, incurable, and progressive diseases. SIMR promotes the following objectives: a greater public understanding of the methods, aims, and benefits of animal research; the provision of the resources necessary for medical research to be conducted; and appropriate legislation relating to medicine and medical research. The group publishes a quarterly newsletter and an annual report.

Bibliography

Books

Lynda Birke and
Ruth Hubbard, eds.

Reinventing Biology: Respect for Life and the Creation of Knowledge. Bloomington: Indiana University Press, 1995.

Peter Carruthers

The Animals Issue: Moral Theory in Practice. New York: Cambridge University Press, 1992.

Stephen R.L. Clark

Animals and Their Moral Standing. New York: Routledge, 1997.

Vernon Coleman

Why Animal Experiments Must Stop. Lynmouth, England: European Medical Journal, 1994.

Marian Dawkins

Through Our Eyes Only?: The Search for Animal Consciousness. New York: W.H. Freeman, 1993.

Alix Fano

Lethal Laws: Animal Testing, Human Health, and Environmental Policy. New York: Zed Books, 1997.

Lawrence Finsen
and Susan Finsen

The Animal Rights Movement in America: From Compassion to Respect. New York: Twayne, 1994.

Raanan Gillon, ed.

Principles of Health Care Ethics. New York: John Wiley, 1994.

Lisa Hepner

Animals in Education: The Facts, Issues, and Implications. Albuquerque, NM: Richmond, 1994.

Gill Langley, ed.

Animal Experimentation: The Consensus Changes. New York: Chapman and Hall, 1989.

Ingrid Newkirk

Free the Animals! The Inside Story of the Animal Liberation Front and Its Founder, "Valerie." Chicago: Noble Press, 1992.

F. Barbara Orlans
et al.

The Human Use of Animals: Case Studies in Ethical Choice. New York: Oxford University Press, 1998.

Evelyn B. Pluhar

Beyond Prejudice: The Moral Significance of Human and Nonhuman Animals. Durham, NC: Duke University Press, 1995.

Rod Preece and
Lorna Chamberlain

Animal Welfare and Human Values. Waterloo, Canada: Wilfrid Laurier University Press, 1993.

Rosemary Rodd

Biology, Ethics, and Animals. New York: Oxford University Press, 1990.

Robert Sharpe

The Cruel Deception: The Use of Animals in Medical Research. Wellingborough, England: Thorson's, 1988.

Peter Singer, ed.

In Defense of Animals. New York: Blackwell, 1985.

Periodicals

Frank Ahrens

"Why Is This Rat Smiling?" *Washington Post*, August 17, 1995. Available from 1150 15th St. NW, Washington, DC 20071.

Pallava Bagla   "Animal Experimentation: Strict Rules Rile Indian Scientists," *Science*, September 18, 1998.

Matt Bai   "Breaking the Cages," *Newsweek*, September 29, 1997.

Neal D. Barnard and Stephen R. Kaufman   "Animal Research Is Wasteful and Misleading," *Scientific American*, February 1997.

Jack H. Botting and Adrian R. Morrison   "Animal Research Is Vital to Medicine," *Scientific American*, February 1997.

Bill Breen   "Why We Need Animal Testing," *Garbage*, April/May 1993. Available from 435 Ninth St., Brooklyn, NY 11215.

Susan Brink   "Clashing Passions: Animal Rights vs. Medical Research," *U.S. News & World Report*, May 4, 1998.

Linda C. Cork et al.   "The Costs of Animal Research: Origins and Options," *Science*, May 2, 1997.

Tony Dajer   "Monkeying with the Brain," *Discover*, January 1992.

P.J. Drucker   "Animal Rights and Wrongs: Teenagers' Views," *Sassy*, May 9, 1996.

Mary Lisa Gavenas   "Animal Testing and Cosmetics," *Glamour*, September 1993.

Anna Maria Gillis   "Toxicity Tests Minus Animals?" *BioScience*, March 1993.

Christine Gorman   "Medicine: What's It Worth to Find a Cure?" *Time*, July 8, 1996.

Judith Hampson   "The Secret World of Animal Experiments," *New Scientist*, April 11, 1992. Available from IPC Specialist Group, King's Reach Tower, Stamford St., London SE1 9LS, England.

Harold A. Herzog Jr.   "Human Morality and Animal Research," *American Scholar*, Summer 1993.

Claire O'Brien   "Yellow Light for Pig-Human Transplants," *Science*, March 8, 1996.

Dick Pothier   "Animal Tests Saved My Life," *Newsweek*, February 1, 1993.

Susan Reed and Sue Carswell   "Controversy: Activist Ingrid Newkirk Fights Passionately for the Rights of Animals; Some Critics Say Humans May Suffer," *People Weekly*, October 22, 1990.

Harriet Ritvo   "Toward a More Peaceable Kingdom," *Technology Review*, April 1992.

Wade Roush   "Hunting for Animal Alternatives," *Science*, October 11, 1996.

Julia Schulhof   "Cosmetics with a Conscience," *American Health*, November 1993.

Richard C. Thompson   "Reducing the Need for Animal Testing," *FDA Consumer*, February 1, 1988.

Wendeline L. Wagner   "They Shoot Monkeys, Don't They?" *Harper's*, August 1997.

Index